WHEN SATAN RULED THE EARTH

Book I

by

M. J. Kelley II

Copyright 2022 ,
All rights reserved.

Formatted, Converted, and Distributed by eBookIt.com
http://www.eBookIt.com

ISBN-13: 978-1-4566-3937-2 (paperback)
ISBN-13: 978-1-4566-3938-9 (ebook)

No part of this book may be reproduced in any form or by any electronic or mechanical means including information storage and retrieval systems, without permission in writing from the author. The only exception is by a reviewer, who may quote short excerpts in a review.

Contents

Preface 1

Prologue 5

Chapter One 7

Chapter Two 11

Chapter Three 23

Chapter Four 37

Chapter Five 51

Chapter Six 69

Chapter Seven 81

Chapter Eight 107

Afterword 125

Table of Authorities 127

Depictions of Shields, Weapons, and Armor: 128

Preface

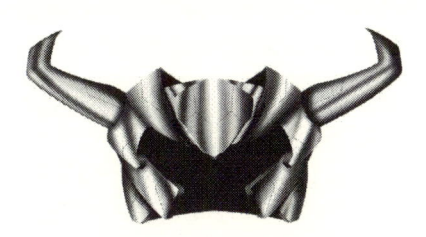

Creation came in three stages: the Heavens and all the angels, then the earth and first humans, and finally the flood and cleansing, which became necessary due to the fallen angels, and which then led to the renewed earth.

However, wasn't it supposed to be perfect right from the start - earth? First Heaven amongst the Three Heavens. Mankind in God's image - a peaceful and beautiful paradise. Only devotion and love for God, His Son, and Holy Spirit should have mattered, which God would return to bless all of mankind for eternity.

What happened?

God had provided free will for all of the angels who had lived peacefully within their own Heaven for an eternity before earth was created. They worshiped Abba, Yeshua, and Eliezer: *God, His Son, and Holy Spirit.*

Then, with the creation of earth, and with mankind to come soon after, some of the angels became jealous: they could not reconcile their feelings of being replaced and abandoned by Abba.

Although this was not the case, they chose to see it this way, and because of this, they lost their love for God.

The archangels built their forces and took one side or the other, and a battle ensued between these rebelling angelic forces and those of the angels remaining loyal to Abba. For a while, it seemed like nothing was going the way God had planned within the history of his Kingdom.

Or was it going just as He had planned all along?

This period of time, or this GAP, between the creation of earth and mankind before Noah's flood, and then the rebirth of earth and mankind thereafter, is the very reason we have the earth and the entirety of mankind as we know them today.

This GAP period provides the reasons for how our perfect paradise was changed in an instant once Lucifer fell. It is supported by evidence of another great flood before Noah's time, when God cleansed the earth from the disease, decay, and detrimental forces of Lucifer and his fallen angels; along with all they had planned to do to corrupt the earth and mankind.

How had this happened, and did God Himself really plan on this right from the beginning of all time?

Had He known what was to occur?

Lucifer returned to earth, along with his legions, just before mankind was created. They were waiting in the wings ready to pounce and to turn mankind against their former Father - *Abba Himself.*

Why had God allowed this?

For His own reasons: His knowledge and wisdom being far superior to our own, it was to ensure that each soul be perfected along its path to Him through exposure *to a corrupted earth: a Hell on earth,* if you will allow me.

One must ask, *why would He plan for such things? What possible good reason could come from all of the disease and destruction of mankind in his new home…?*

Turns out, it was to be the only reason that would ever truly matter.

For what good is the devotion of a soul if it is not aware of an alternative purpose, direction, and meaning in life? How could God provide salvation when a soul only knows its duty to worship, praise, and to love God in Three Persons?

Would not salvation be better, and more rewarding, if eternally begotten through a choice born of knowledge, free will, and then a willing return to worship of the one who had given birth to all life right from the very beginning?

And so, it came to pass, that upon the earth, mankind invented and found many distractions that would take most away from their sole objective. *Why is this so? Was love not enough for us?*

Weren't we primarily meant for loving and being loved by God only?

That did not work the first time ... when angels were the only creations, and love and free will mixed together until love itself had become worthy of being questioned by those whose devotion fell short of where it was to be.

God knew what He was doing all along. It was just a matter of learning the fate of those who chose disloyalty.

We now have the answers as to how these forces collided in the heavens and how they came to be upon the face of the earth. We know it altered our history and our relationship with God once and for all time.

This series is a roadmap distilled from all of the possibilities of God's creation of earth and mankind, and it becomes a trajectory of our creation history.

So, begin to read and to understand our place within God's Kingdom, now and for always. It is all here, told in plain language, in the form of a story:

GAP Book One.

Prologue

In the beginning God created the heaven and the earth (Genesis 1:1).[1]

Earth was supposed to be the perfect world, the first heaven, full of life and with man created out of the earth, whose purpose was to live joyfully and peacefully while worshiping God.

However, before God created earth, according to His plan, He would first create three billion Bene-Elohim, Sons of God, who were to be subordinate angels, and who were to be ruled over by three Archangels. Each Archangel would have under his command one billion of the Bene-Elohim, and each soul would have its perfect place in the order Abba had intended. There would be Messenger Archangel Gabriel, the Warrior Archangel Michael, and finally, Worshiper Archangel Lucifer.

Gabriel, Michael, and Lucifer, along with the three billion Bene-Elohim, would all live peacefully together in what would be originally the first heaven. Each of the Archangels would assure that the subordinate angels and spiritual beings beneath their command remained dutiful, prayerful, and worshipful towards Abba, Yeshua, and Eliezer.

---

[1] All Bible verses, references regarding the angels, and references for certain passages of dialogue throughout the text were taken from Bible Gateway, King James Version. https://www.biblegateway.com/versions/King-James-Version-KJV-Bible/

Second heaven was saved for God the Father, Abba, God the Son, Yeshua, and God the Spirit, Eliezer, and was to be the Most-High place. Everything and each soul was to have its place in God's perfect order to all life.

And after having created these sons of God, Abba would have the idea to create the first heaven, earth, where he would put man. The angels would remain in their heaven, but it would thereafter be called the second heaven. God The Father (Abba), God the Son (Yeshua), God the Spirit (Eliezer), would remain in the Most-High place, which would thereafter be called the third heaven.

All would go very well, according to Abba's idea - after all, the angels were Bene-Elohim, sons of God, whose sole purpose was to love, honor, and respect Abba, Yeshua, and Eliezer, and to accept their places along with the decisions of the Triune Elohim. Abba saw it all and it was good, and his plans for earth, along with creating man in His own image, was exciting. He would have far many more souls to love. The angels could not be replaced, and nor should they have any qualms. Gabriel and Michael lauded Abba's decisions. All was fine and upright amongst the archangels and the three billion subordinate angels.

Until one rebelled ….

Chapter One

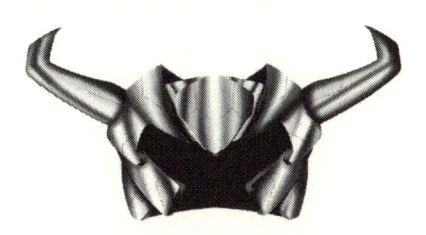

Abba turned to face his Son, Yeshua. "Let us create!"

In his splendid white robe, Yeshua looked at God. "Yes, Abba, it is time. Let's."

Raising his vast right hand, suddenly first heaven appeared just beneath them, filling the dark void that had been forever. It was beautiful and majestic, endless, serene, and warm.

Eliezer looked and saw that it was so. "It is good."

"We shall have Bene-Elohim, what I will call *angels*," Abba said. "They are to be my sons, and I shall love and cherish them for eternity."

"Let it be done according to Thy will," Yeshua said.

With a wave of his left hand, and then a shock of might from his right hand, souls too numerous to count filled first heaven. The three looked down upon first heaven and saw endless fields of finest grass with no boundaries. Blue skies, puffy white clouds, and three billion new souls all getting accustomed to spontaneous life.

Eliezer spoke. "And now, the three special angels, Abba. Remember, the idea was to have three in charge of the rest."

"Yes, and it shall be so." Abba held out his right hand and the thought was so. Suddenly, three new Bene-Elohim came into existence in first heaven. Abba spoke to each. "You are to be my Messenger, *Archangel Gabriel*." He turned to the second. "And you will be the *Warrior Archangel Michael*." Finally, he looked with joy at the third. "And you, my *Worshiper Archangel Lucifer*. Each of the three billion souls you see are now beneath your command. Each is to have their perfect place and order in your home, which we have named *First Heaven*, as I have intended."

Now Yeshua spoke to each of the three billion and three Bene-Elohim. "We remain here in Second Heaven, which is beautiful beyond any description that you might understand, with a view overlooking everything Abba has created for you and which is now in existence in First Heaven."

"We will remain here in Second Heaven," Abba said. "Which will be only for Abba, Yeshua, and Eliezer for now. None of the Bene-Elohim will be permitted to be here, however, you will want for nothing in First Heaven."

Eliezer had a thought, which penetrated each of the souls in First Heaven all at the same time. "We are here and we love you, and you were created just to enjoy the love we have for you. Yes, we hope to have your love for all time. Your role is to worship and to honor, love, and obey Abba, his son Yeshua, and me, Eliezer, who is the Spirit of love itself."

At the command of the three Archangels, each of the three billion Bene-Elohim fell to their knees and extended their arms out above them towards Second Heaven. The souls, whether they be the three archangels themselves, or any of the three billion subordinate angels, had been made in God's image. Like Him, they could walk, float, hover, sit, lay down, or kneel.

Abba waved his right arm and then there was manna and drink in Second Heaven for the Bene-Elohim. They got up from kneeling and began to inhabit their home. They were weightless and could eat as much manna and drink as much ale as they wanted to without ever gaining weight. Rest was a constant circumstance - sleep was unheard of and not necessary. When the Elohim spoke, each listened intently and could hear without distraction.

The angels' role in worshiping Elohim and living peacefully was done with the sole purpose of loving, praising, and worshiping the Triune God. So long as half of their time was spent praising Abba, endless graces were given to all of the angels, who had not a care or concern. Discomfort, illness, fatigue, and distress were unknown, not even a thought. They never worried about favorites, as each had their unique role and their special place in Abba's perfect construction of their world.

Occasionally, some one or other of the angels would suggest to the others how much they would enjoy being able to see Second Heaven. Lucifer would tell them, "You have all you need here. No need to go to Second Heaven. Abba has already told you that place is not for you, but for them."

An angel beneath his command named Joash turned to Lucifer. "Would it be so harmful for us to have a glimpse of Second Heaven to see how wonderful it is?"

Lucifer laughed. "Why would you want anything more when you have so much all around you?" He waved his hands out in all directions and Joash looked around First Heaven.

Then Midian, who loved Abba, Yeshua, and Eliezer above all of the angels, said rather sternly, "Yes, Lucifer is correct, Joash. No need for us to go to Second Heaven. Perhaps you should go to your knees now as Abba sees you and knows your thoughts. Praise Him and love Him now so we do not cause any anger towards us."

Joash's companion was an angel named Jael, who loved Abba, but who seemed to be wanting more than what he had been given already, and certainly much more than what most of the rest of the Bene-Elohim desired. He spoke to Lucifer on Joash's behalf. "You cannot blame Joash for his curiosity. We all feel it from time to time."

Just then, Archangel Gabriel came to their space. He looked at the three angels and then at Lucifer. "I bring a message from Yeshua. We are about to prepare for council and worship."

"Just in time," Lucifer said, looking with disdain first at Joash, and then turning to Jael.

With that, all souls in Second Heaven fell to their knees to listen to the Elohim.

Chapter Two

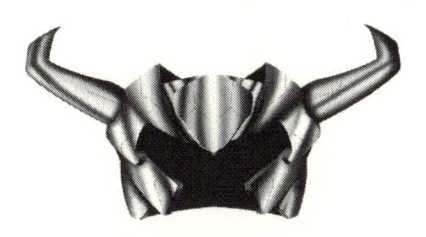

Just before the council began, Abba was with Yeshua and Eliezer discussing their works thus far.

Abba looked at his Son and said, "We have given the angels free will, for what soul could love, and of what value would be that love, if souls were made to worship without having a choice? By giving each soul free will, we are assured that the love they have for us is true, and not given for the sake of mere obligation or in hopes of getting something in return."

Eliezer was spirit alone, without form, and his thoughts were transmissible upon the instantaneous presumption of His will. He always listened and accounted for Abba's and Yeshua's words. Similarly, He could focus at any time on any of the three billion and three angels' thoughts, but would do so customarily when they were directed towards the Triune Elohim. He spoke thus, in thought without words, to Abba and Yeshua, "It is good and true. Free will encompasses those goals. Yet the risk is some will come to rely upon their own strengths in lieu of prayer and devotion to us three."

"Yes," Abba said. "Truth."

"I have seen, amongst others, an unnecessary need to lead, which compels those close to them to feel the desire to challenge the archangels," Yeshua added.

"Yes, and then more feel it is important for them to try doing the same," Eliezer made clear.

Abba seemed unfazed by these disclosures. He smiled and spoke. "Wanting more than what has been allotted was my first expectation.

Love does not seem to sustain those, and so then their own boredom of purpose becomes unsettling to them."

Eliezer's tone became one of alarm. "With these three identifiable manifestations of corruption, it is likely that eventually, some angels will need an intervention by their commanding archangel before they go off in their own deluded search."

"Deluded searches will become the folly for those who cannot take our love and give due worship and praise back," Abba exclaimed. "There can be no other way for these such angels."

"We've given them life, yet how is it possible that all will not eventually realize that their value and true worth comes only from Us?" Eliezer questioned.

"It is all in my great plan," Abba said. "Free will brings with it a burden of temptation. Each angel is fully equipped with everything necessary to make correct choices."

"Though some will not," Yeshua interjected.

Abba continued, "Although it is true that they are equal, except for the abundance of powers we have granted the three archangels, I have foreseen that those who love each other as they love us, will not have the burden brought on by the need to take control or compete with others. Those who cannot learn to love each and every other will therefore be swayed by their own boredom of purpose, and so will feel the need to compete and lead others wrongfully."

"For love itself *surely is enough*," Eliezer added.

Yeshua understood. "I see it is those who have not yet learned to love all others who will have a lengthy battle in front of them." Feeling the truth of His Father's words, and realizing the wisdom of having given free will, Yeshua declared, "Abba is correct. There can be no other way."

Abba nodded, "With Michael, Gabriel, and Lucifer as my commanders, those who do not wish to be satisfied with what we have provided them will be watched carefully. The three will report back to us what is taking some souls away from their duty to honor and love."

Eliezer had a thought which immediately went to Abba and Yeshua.

Abba said, "Yes, it is good. We shall provide each soul with armor and I shall give my commanders, and their chosen soldiers, weapons in order to provide assurance of their authority granted by us over the remaining."

"Meantime," Yeshua added, "my hope is in the goodness inherent in free will for most of the angels - that each will value what they have and will be satisfied, without being driven by the desire to become furthermore powerful, and as such, then manipulate other angels for their own gain."

"We shall see what will come," Eliezer transmitted.

There was a pause between them as they considered all of the possibilities. Then Abba stood and looked closely into the doings within First Heaven. "There will be many transitions to come. We shall see change, conflict, and what will be the most amazing thing of all - how each handles this burden. Some will succeed and others will fail, but many will be caught in-between. Those will have to recommit to us if they finally decide to properly align their allegiances with the Triune."

"How could anything else compare to the power of Our love, Abba?" Yeshua asked.

He answered. "Once created, when giving them volition, creation is then set free from Our hands. First came the interactions between each of the angels and their habitat, First Heaven. But more importantly, came their interactions with *each other*. For those not relying upon their devotions to the Triune, being surrounded in their heaven with other angels causes the undevoted an instantaneous reaction which changes their very being."

"Those feel the temptation of their own power," Eliezer suggested. "They feel invincible and as if, on their own, they are quite capable of life and happiness."

Abba said, "All angels by necessity will feel everything each of the others feel. All know what is required of them, and yet they will become opposed to that due to the influence of, and their attraction to, the ones who proclaim the goodness of their own power."

"Once again, I can see quite clearly the sum of Our wisdom. Yes, I agree, there can be no other way," Eliezer answered. "Free will, as such, includes destructive forces."

Yeshua said, "And yet, all that it would take for those who turn away, is for them to bring their will back into alignment with Ours. That they have free will, only they themselves can return it to its rightful owner and be forgiven. If they do, then those who do so will be just fine."

"They will remain in First Heaven, and one day, First and Second Heaven will be joined, and all of Us shall live together, those who have been tested and found true, along with the Triune," Abba confirmed.

"I see now," Yeshua answered. "Some will be stubborn and stiff-necked, falsely believing in their own powers, or in the powers of one of the others. This will be a long process to sort out, and for those who turn and make it back, it will become a very turbulent and trying path which they will have chosen to take."

"Yes," Abba said.

"Yes," Eliezer agreed.

"I see free will then as a burden, not a gift. It has the potential to fool many with its affinity for pride," Yeshua said. "Yes, Abba, it is a necessary trait in that it will reveal to us who will be our true servants, but also, it will identify who will turn from us once and for all."

Abba nodded. "I will give them one more angel as an example to them of their true mission of purpose. He will fly with wings and sit high in First Heaven, and he will have but one purpose - that of praising the Triune. His title will be 'The *Seraphim!*'"

And with that, council began.

On the upper throne made of brilliant gold, Abba sat, while Yeshua took a smaller throne to his right, also made of solid gold. Eliezer was there between them, as noted by a glowing red orb with shining white rays of pure, vibrant warmth coming down all the way into First Heaven. From First Heaven, every angel could see them as if they were just out of reach. Yeshua was in full view, as always, and similarly, Abba's face was hidden from their sight, this time by a golden veil.

However, his voice could be heard clearly, and Abba spoke to his angels. "As you have come to have life in abundance, you will come to learn that We are not yet through with creating. I am pleased with you, and yet I notice some of you have a penchant for dissatisfaction with Our creation as a whole. Remember, nothing goes unnoticed."

Yeshua would always listen and then help to communicate along with Abba, interpreting and clarifying, while supporting the angels. He said to them, "What is a gift if it is not valued? How so then, your very existence?"

And Eliezer watched and His role would be to interject his thoughts directly into the minds and hearts of all present, every living soul in existence at that time. "There is order and praise, both of which are very pleasing to Us. If you feel otherwise, then you must know you are finding your own way. Be careful, for finding your own way is a path wrought with temptation to veer away from what you have each been called to do."

"As such," Abba said. "I now create *The Seraphim!*"

The angels watched in amazement as Abba's right hand thrust forward and spun until a glowing sphere of intense light came from out of nowhere in the space before Him. The light chased itself in circles until a figure appeared, a completely new soul, dazzling in sight and presence before all of the angels.

He had six wings of large golden feathers, he appeared otherwise in the same form as the angels, and he immediately knelt before the Triune Elohim. *"Holy, holy, holy ... Holy, holy, holy...."* He sang in rich and luxurious tones replete with sadness, hope, joy, and honor all at once. *"Holy, holy, holy ... Holy, holy, holy...."* The more they listened to the Seraphim, their hearts felt great longing to be unified in totality to Abba, Yeshua, and Eliezer. The melodic voice transported them to a state of mind which flourished in worship. All the angels watched him for quite some time, until it was clear the Seraphim was meant for this one purpose only - he was meant to continue singing God's praises like this for all time, and in so doing, to remind the angels of their purpose in creation.

Archangel Lucifer turned to his friend Archangel Gabriel. "An angel meant to worship and praise, and to perform that one task only for all time."

"Yes," Gabriel answered. "Is it not wonderful? He is meant to be a model for the other angels and to help them with the duty of worship."

Lucifer nodded, but seemed a bit puzzled. Of all the angels, The Triune had made Lucifer a bit taller and more powerful than the others. Gabriel and the third archangel, Michael, were of similar stature to the remaining three billion angels; whereas Lucifer, meant from the beginning of time to be the worshiping angel, was to stand out to the rest. And so he did: Lucifer was created by Abba to have half as much more presence than the remaining angels.

"I do not know why some of the angels under my command seem despondent at times, like they oblige out of duty and not out of love," Lucifer said to Gabriel, an obvious flash of pain crossing his face. "I have tried my best to have the angels under my command to perform this function as dutifully as had been expected by Abba. I am frustrated at their lack of love when I see some that are falling short. I feel responsible, and I wish I could do more."

"Patience, Lucifer," Gabriel said. "The Father knows our needs."

"Yet, at times, it seems clear He likes us to suffer the weaknesses of others."

"It may seem so, but that cannot be true."

Lucifer watched the Seraphim, allowing his voice to penetrate into his soul. "I would rather be that Seraphim than be in charge of angels who honor only themselves."

"Surely there cannot be that many who are self-involved?"

"If there be a billion, surely ten thousand of them."

"I don't believe I have that many marauders beneath my own command." Gabriel smiled at Lucifer and watched the pain melt from his face. "Let us listen to see if He has some plans in mind to help us."

"I trust in Him," Lucifer said, "but perhaps it would be best to devise our own plans. My angels, as I have said, have been somewhat despondent lately. So, a secondary plan may be in order."

"You doubt the word of our Father?" Gabriel gazed at Lucifer, his expression cool. But inside, doubt wormed its way in and Gabriel noticed it felt like an ugly, putrid feeling. Never before had any of the angels deviated from Abba's plan. After all, why would they?

"No, of course not," Lucifer said. "I merely wish to have several plans ready, in case the worst should happen. And, I care for the lives of my soldiers, as any proper general would."

At this, Gabriel nodded in understanding.

Lucifer did not wish to go against Him, or deviate from his plan. Lucifer was simply the cautious sort, a fine quality to have for a commander of Abba's armies.

"And, as though it may stand, I simply do not trust this Seraphim just yet," Lucifer continued, and Gabriel jerked his head back in confusion. Lucifer raised a brow. "My friend, I mean no harm, nor insult to Him, but all of this raises a question, does it not?"

"It does? Just what do you mean by that, Lucifer?"

"Soldiers, armies, *us,*" Lucifer pressed. "We are warriors, down to our core. So that, in turn, begs the question. What is the purpose of an army, if not to wage war?"

"Against His enemies," Gabriel returned.

"And when there are no more?" Lucifer asked.

"Peace," Gabriel said, as if he was discussing the weather. "Obviously."

"My friend," Lucifer placed his hand on Gabriel's shoulder. "You and I both know that for beings like us, there will never be any peace."

"I'm afraid I do not understand," Gabriel frowned. "What is it that you mean Lucifer, truly?"

Lucifer said nothing, and his eyes flickered. Patting his friend's shoulder once, Lucifer faced Abba, who began to speak once more.

"Upon this day, I bequeath to you, my sons, my warriors all, arms, and armor, to shield you from this coming war." Yeshua and Eliezer were somewhat taken aback with Abba's mention of war.

Suddenly, a living light flashed in His palm, and then, from the width of Second Heaven itself, came the armor of the Divine. Made in celestial metals that defied anything any of the angels had seen before, solid gold and silver, meant to ward off any aggressive tool or device, came suits of armor and shields gently descending upon all of the angels. Each one took their offered gifts, and as Archangels Lucifer and Gabriel accepted theirs, they looked over their newly acquired gifts with a mixture of hesitation and awe.

In their hands rested armor that would shield them for the coming days. Emblazoned with two symbols, the shields themselves had the Aleph on its right side. The Aleph was meant to represent obedience to Abba, and praise for him with all their heart. It was to remind the angels of their duty and of the Triune's presence for all eternity and it had a bending lower elliptical oval with two horns coming out above it. The Tav, which was a cross of solid silver, was a mark and symbol of truth, perfection, and completion, and this was on the left side of every shield.

Along with shields, the angels had each received a helmet covering their entire head and extending out across their cheeks, along with complete body armor, covering their feet, legs, hands, and arms, all made of solid gold and silver.

And then came their weaponry.

Lucifer glanced to find a floating blade in front of Grabiel, who was too engrossed in his armor to notice. Gently, he smacked his elbow into Gabriel, who glanced at him, then at the sword in front of him. The blade was of suitable length for an Angel of Gabriel's size, a large, two-handed, double-edged sword that shone with gleaming gold on its handle.

As Gabriel peered at the blade, he saw it was solid ice, but that when he put it down into its blackened sheath, the flicker of flames sparked across the ice, and as he retook hold of it, divine flames burst from its hilt, flowing upwards and encasing the blade in a wreath of fire. He held it high up towards Abba.

"Amazing," Gabriel said, his voice hushed.

"Indeed," Lucifer nodded. "You hold it well."

Gabriel glanced at his oldest friend, and nodded. "Thank you, but what about you? I see no weapon that will lay upon your hands."

Lucifer opened his mouth to reply, then glanced upwards. Gabriel followed his gaze, but while armor, shields, swords, and bows and arrows were settling down upon the three billion angels, and yet, not one weapon was given to Lucifer. He stood there, silent, and waiting for his turn. *And yet, nothing came.*

At least, at first.

Then, his fears lifted, and slowly, gently, flying down to his hands was a spear. An ornate weapon, made of gold and silver that matched the color scheme given to the other angels. Lucifer gently raised his hand, and took the weapon in hand. It was of good weight, not too light, not too heavy. Just right.

And yet, Lucifer found it unsatisfactory.

In the back of his mind, Lucifer was willing to entertain the notion that he, of all the Archangels, of all of Abba's forces and all of his men, did not need such paltry things such as a spear, a peasant's weapon, to perform his duty. Such a mere tool was beneath him, and it was better off in the hands of someone who needed it more. A weaker angel, perhaps.

He entertained that notion, but even so, as the divine light faded, and a chorus of voices marveled at their gifts, and yet mummers of disappointment and frustration ran through the crowds. Lucifer found some solace in the fact that he wasn't alone in his anger.

He entertained the notion, but he did not believe it.

"Are you alright, my friend?" Gabriel asked.

"Of course," Lucifer replied, his tone firm, but the foundations shaken. "Why wouldn't I be?"

"You seem…distraught," Gabriel said. "Are you, perhaps, dissatisfied with your gift? A spear seems to be a mighty weapon, so why do you seem to dislike it?"

Lucifer, for the first time in his long life, struggled to find the words. "I…I believe I am meant to wield something greater. A spear, while fine, is not to my tastes."

Lucifer told himself it was because, as a creature of flight, a spear would be difficult to use in personal combat, where he could meet his foes head on. Especially in mass combat, where there wasn't a lot of room to work with. In flight, then perhaps his spear would be able to find his mark, but what if the enemy approached from behind, or otherwise managed to grasp the shaft?

A spear would be good for dive-bombing the enemy, but little else for an Archangel of his size. But more than that, it was a weapon used by foot soldiers, by the common angels. Perhaps it was to help spread a message of unity, but Lucifer was not a common angel. *He was the first among a billion, and he had to stand out from them.*

Had Abba chosen poorly? Lucifer banished the thought as soon as it arrived, but, even so…

"I rather like it," Gabriel said. "It suits you well, my friend."

It was an attempt at comfort, but to Lucifer, Gabriel may as well have smacked him in the face. "Thank you," Lucifer said with a forced smile, and shook his head. "Come then, let us meet with our kin, and rejoice in the gifts offered, we have much to do now."

"Agreed," Gabriel said, and the two donned their armor, grasped their shields and weapons, and then set off together back into the halls of First Heaven.

Gabriel, as they walked together, basking in the gifts given to them, glanced at his friend's face, which was set in a steady scowl. Gabriel wanted to believe that his friend's troubles were in passing, that Lucifer's feelings would fade, and the happy future would be shared by the both of them.

He wanted to, but he did not believe it.

Something had changed ....

Chapter Three

In the First Heaven, very few things ended, as blessed by Abba as they were. However, even among such eternity, there were few things stronger than the friendship between Lucifer and Gabriel, save for the latter's devotion to their father.

As the two walked down their gilded halls, a question arose in Lucifer's mind, and he regarded his friend, nay, his brother, with a simple question.

"What," he began, "is the first thing you're going to do when His plan is done?"

"Serve Him faithfully, of course," Gabriel replied.

"Yes, of course," Lucifer nodded, "but what else? What do you think your duties will be, exactly?"

It was a simple question, but Gabriel, in all of his years of experience, had no true answer for it. "I…will follow His plan, of course," Gabriel said, then nodded. "Oh, I see, do you wish to inquire how I will?"

Lucifer hesitated for a moment, then nodded. "Sure."

"I will watch over His creatures and creations to the best of my ability, and strike down any who would dare harm them," he said.

"Even," Lucifer crossed his arms. "If it was me?"

Gabriel focused his eyes. *"Even you."*

The two stared silently at each other for a moment, before breaking out into laughter. Their comradery was easy, shared. The kind forged over years of working, praying, and living together. It was one that both Gabriel and Lucifer enjoyed, and after all this time, they could share each other's doubts, and misgivings, about their tasks without fear of judgment or disappointment. Simply put, they were best friends.

As their laughter ceased, Lucifer nodded. "So, tell me Gabriel, how does your armor weigh upon you? Not too light, I hope?"

"I believe mine might be the heaviest of them all, and unequaled," Gabriel replied. "I have yet to test its divine strength, though."

"Hm," Lucifer thought for a moment. "So, you wish to throw yourself into the fire, so to speak?"

Gabriel paused, then nodded. "I would throw myself into the sun if He asked it of me."

Lucifer shook his head, and placed a hand on Gabriel's shoulder. "Not quite what I meant, my friend, but good to know."

Gabriel then realized what his friend was getting at. He looked at Lucifer with a mischievous smile. "Tussle, then?"

"I thought you might never ask!" Lucifer replied, and with that, he raised his spear and Gabriel immediately raised his sword aloft, setting the air between them ablaze with the fire emanating from the blade of his sword. Lucifer smiled, and leveled his spear. To each, their unique weapon's weight was unfamiliar, but this was the perfect opportunity to give them a try and gain some useful experience.

Lucifer moved first, dashing forward in a blur of motion as he extended his spear forward. Gabriel, unused to the heft of his new sword, made a clumsy block that only barely served to deflect the blow, but in an instant, Gabriel darted forward and into Lucifer's reach. At this range, he was unable to bring the blade itself to bear, but the pommel worked just fine. A fact proven as Gabriel thrust the handle forward, right into Lucifer's shoulder. Staggering back, Lucifer half grinned, while at the same time, gritted his teeth. *The first full contact blow went to Gabriel.*

At this time, they began the duel proper. Dancing in circles with weapons whistling swiftly around themselves and each other, the blades of each weapon flashed in heaven's light - Lucifer with his divine gold and silver spear, and Gabriel with his sword of ice and flames. Each was naturally adept using their shields to deflect incoming jabs by the other. In fact, the clanking and whooshing sounds of weapons hitting the shields was constant, and it drew the keen interest of more than a few onlookers.

To those who came to observe, it may have appeared that the two were dancing. Each movement, each twist of the arm with its coordinated and complementary footwork, was as graceful and perfectly-timed as the cherubims' singing their songs of love and praise to Abba. As one gave a blow, the other deflected and converted the energy back with yet another strike. There was ferocity in their movements, but rather than intent to deliver a piercing blow, there was a mutual recognition of temperance.

Lucifer was spurred on by his pride and the desire to impress his friend, and yet he soon realized that with such a weapon, if complemented with his skillfulness, and dare he consider the emotion of rage, *he would be unstoppable*. Gabriel moved with the goal of not surpassing, or even defeating, Lucifer. Rather, he fought to surpass *himself* by becoming a better soldier than he currently considered himself to be. *For he was one of Abba's angels, and in order to serve, he must be ready.*

At very least, the two were learning and becoming more comfortable with their shields, armor, and weaponry. As they gazed into each other's eyes while in the heat of combat, each also learned a valuable lesson about reading the movements and intent of their foe. Lucifer could tell Gabriel felt a bit more unease with combat than he himself did, and this caused him to believe he was the far better warrior, even as Gabriel's sword hit the armor of his right shoulder. To prove his own untested insight, Lucifer did a quick dance, spin, and thrust, coming around full circle and with his spearhead in perfect alignment with Gabriel's exposed right flank. He flicked by him with the spearhead's trio of blades, and Gabriel was unable to deflect it this time.

Lucifer looked at Gabriel and smiled. "Got you, my friend."

Soon enough, their duel ended, and both put their weapons to rest.

"Well done," Gabriel said. "By the third stroke, I could not see your lance."

"But you found it nonetheless," Lucifer returned.

"Ah," Gabriel patted the side of his head, an inch away from his eyes. "You give away what you were going to do with your eyes."

Lucifer snorted. *"I don't think I am the only one who did so!"*

Gabriel raised a hand to his armor, checking to see if any damage had occurred. Lucifer followed his gaze. Much to the surprise of both, it nary had a nick. "I must admit, this armor has its uses," Lucifer said.

Gabriel nodded. "And you? I trust you find yours well?"

Lucifer looked at his own armor. "I do, though I have to admit, I find the colors a bit…"

"Do you dislike them?" Gabriel asked. "I'm rather fond of the gold and silver, myself."

"No, no, not at all," Lucifer cut in. "I simply…hm?" He tilted his head, gazing past Gabriel, who turned to follow his gaze. There, another pair of angels stood facing each other, fists clenched and glaring. They circled each other like animals, and their body language screamed out one word: *attack*. With their shields and weaponry tossed aside, their faces twisted into snarls, and their teeth were bared.

"This," one jabbed at the other, *"is your fault."*

"Mine?" the other recoiled. "I'm not the one who goes against His plan!"

Lucifer swiftly moved past his friend with hurried desperation. "Soldiers!" he barked, and the two angels snapped to attention at once on pure instinct. Gabriel approached shortly thereafter, just as Lucifer recognized these angels as beneath his own command due to the narrow red line across their foreheads. "What," Lucifer began, "is the meaning of this? *Are you not brothers?"*

"No," the first one spat. "I may be an angel, but I alone decide my kin."

"Except," Gabriel cut in, "for our Father."

The angel said nothing, but his lips tightened.

"Again, why are you two acting like this? You were about to come to blows, what is the cause ... *the reason?*" Lucifer demanded.

"The reason?" the second angel growled. "This....interloper has begun to whisper doubts among the troops."

"Doubts?" Lucifer echoed.

"Yes," the second angel answered with a nod of his head.

"Before that," Gabriel interrupted with a frown. "Names. *Now.*"

"Zered," the first angel said.

"Asher," the second angel answered.

Lucifer nodded. "Asher, Zered, I want *both* of you to explain what exactly is going on here. Then, I shall see if a punishment is necessary."

"A punishment?" Zered protested. "Sir, are we not required to speak nothing but the truth? Are we not meant to speak our minds, lest we embark down a trail of lies?"

Lucifer frowned. "Besides some allegation of spreading doubt, neither of you two have explained what is going on, and I expect a proper reason, *now.*"

His tone booked no argument, and Asher nodded. "I have heard whispers among the ranks of disobedience to Him. These angels seem to be distraught." Lifting his hand and pointing at the angel in front of him, he continued. "I have seen this angel converse with others whose gifts, if I may be so bold, *have been lacking.*"

"And you?" Lucifer looked to Zered, "Are these whispers true?"

"Sir," Zered said. "While I love our father... I truly do, am I not beholden to my own thoughts, *my own will?* Surely there is nothing wrong with expressing my discontent amongst my fellows."

"Have you taken any action against Him?" Lucifer asked.

"No," Zered answered.

"Then, Asher," Lucifer focused on the second angel. "There is nothing I can do. Though I understand your worries, whispers and want are not punishable crimes."

"*But, sir....*"

"I believe we should investigate regardless," Gabriel cut in, glancing at Lucifer and then quickly back at Asher. "As you well know, even a cinder can start a fire."

Asher seemed pleased.

Lucifer nodded. "Yes, I agree." He peered at Zered with intense scrutiny. "Now, both of you are dismissed. And for each of your sakes, I recommend not seeing each other for a bit of time, *if at all.*"

The two nodded, and then picked up their shields and weapons. Before departing, they each sent a daggered glare at the other, and this was noted by Lucifer and Gabriel. As Zered passed by Lucifer, a whisper fell to the wind. "Sir, perhaps you should check your own heart, before you lecture others."

Lucifer frowned as Zered left. Something about his words…was true. Was it a crime to think for oneself? Even when those thoughts led one away from Abba's wishes? Lucifer was uncertain if Gabriel had heard Zered's almost silent lamentation. He quickly glanced at his friend and did his best not to let his concerns show, but Gabriel's brow rose as he scanned Lucifer's face.

Without giving anything away, Gabriel placed his sword back into its sheath. "What troubles await us?" he asked. "That we can no longer trust our own troops?"

"What do you mean?" Lucifer frowned, facing his friend fully.

"As much as I do not wish to believe it, the anger in their eyes was certain," Gabriel continued. They laid back and began floating upwards towards the Kingdom. "I believe I shall ask a few Cherubs to look into this matter. Though I wish it were not so." Though much smaller and quite younger looking, the Cherubim angels were known for their devotion to Abba, Yeshua, and Eliezer. They were within the ranks of each of the three Archangels' legions, and somehow remained above the doings of the other angels. Most notably, they were trusted without question.

Drifting, Gabriel and Lucifer noticed groups of angels in ceremonious celebrations of devotions and worship across the heavens, with drifting white clouds separating the legions. "Yes, that would serve us well. Tell me," Lucifer tilted his head. "Do you believe that there truly will be traitors?"

Gabriel frowned, and then sighed. "It is not a thought I am comfortable with: brother against brother, son of God against son of God, and all of us angels to our cores. If it were up to me, we would have no need of soldiers or fighters, and so then, we could all live in peace with our Father. But, I must be realistic."

"Of course, but to suspect others merely because they disagree?" Lucifer raised a brow. "There is a difference between caution and zealtory, my friend."

They stopped on the outskirts of one of the posts in order to pray. "Of course," Gabriel nodded. "And I hope that disagreements are all that will be found. I believe Michael will have something to say, I will go to see him, and ask him for advice on this subject. I must admit, I lack the golden tongue that you have, or Michael's vision."

"Should I come with you?" Lucifer asked, and Gabriel stared at him for a single moment.

"No," he replied. "I believe I shall tend to this matter alone. You have your prayer service now, and then armies to prepare, do you not?"

Lucifer nodded, and watched his best friend go. As he watched, he couldn't shake the feeling that maybe, just maybe, that Zared had a point.

***

The halls of Heaven were divine, adorned in brilliant light, and vastly spaced upon marble halls that resembled blue sky and white clouds. There were few things in existence that rivaled its majesty, save for Abba himself, his love for his creations, and Archangel Michael's devotion to his purpose.

Michael stood in his study, reviewing lengthy documents that he himself had created since time began for any possible necessity, including the possibility of upcoming battle. He stood a head and a half taller than most, and had a gentle face adorned with flowing red hair that cascaded to the bottom of his neck. His gaze was almost always keen and focused. As he studied, suddenly, his eyes flickered to the doorway in front of him, as if expecting something.

And that expectation was proven justified when Gabriel pushed the door open and strode inside.

"Ah," Michael smiled, "Gabriel, my friend, my brother! Just as I thought to myself that I have not seen you in the last while, as if you had summoned my concerns, here you are in front of me."

"Michael, my brother, it is good to see you here in your customary manner," Gabriel responded, and then paused.

Michael noticed Gabriel's expression was not his typical one of unabashed love and joy. *"What seems to be the matter?"*

"I will admit it bothers me to report what I feel I must." And then Gabriel said with all the subtlety of ten million angels raising their voices in gratitude to Abba all at once, "I have dire news regarding Lucifer, and, I dare to say, those of our kin."

Michael stood from his chair immediately. "...Explain."

Gabriel nodded. "Lucifer and I encountered a pair of angels arguing in the fields. Their names were Asher and Zared, of Lucifer's troops. The gist of it was that...." Gabriel stumbled over his own words, as if it was unconscionable that he had to even get to this point. "Some angels have...*doubts*."

"What sort of doubts," Michael asked.

Shaking his head, Gabriel said, "Doubts regarding *His plan.*"

Michael nodded slowly and as if he had been struck in the chest with a lance. "And what of Lucifer? How did he respond?"

"He inquired of the one just how far these thoughts had gone. They had not turned into action at all."

"And....?"

"Lucifer had them separate and agreed that I should send some of my cherubims to inquire further." Gabriel's shoulders sagged. "Yet, I had the feeling that Lucifer himself had doubts in kind. He almost seemed...convinced by Zared's arguments. Though he did not speak it, it was plain to see on his face."

"Lucifer...." Michael repeated.

"I do not wish to suspect my friend, but...." Gabriel frowned. "But I fear for him. I find myself torn. There have already been reports, or mere rumors, of discontent; and this we don't know for sure. It all makes me uncertain and anxious. What if prayers turn to curses? *What if the worst happens?*"

Michael nodded, crossing his arms as he stepped away from his desk. "That will not happen."

"Are you sure?" Gabriel asked.

Michael said nothing, his eyes flickering from Gabriel to his desk. "...No. To be truthful, I share some of your fears. I too have noticed some...discontentment amongst the ranks. Though why, I cannot say."

"Is the love for and of our Father not enough?" Gabriel asked, and Michael shook his head.

"No, sadly," Michael replied. "If we lived in absolute perfection alone, then the love of one another is all that would be required. I can...," he searched for the words, "... almost understand, I suppose, why there would be discontent among our kin."

"You can?" Gabriel blinked, and Michael at first nodded, and then shook his head.

Michael thought a moment more. "In His love, Abba gave us all free will." He looked at Gabriel until the importance of his words hit home.

Gabriel was, in Michael's humble opinion, a true guardian. Loyal beyond all else, but sadly, his ability to understand why angels sometimes acted out-of-sorts was somewhat lacking. It was adorable, in a way. Gabriel knew who he was, what he wanted, and stuck to what he believed, no matter where it would take him. As stalwart as the pillars of heavens, and just as stubborn. This made him a formidable guardian, a loyal friend, and a capable leader, who guided his troops from the front.

Though Michael also knew that sadly, it meant that the smaller things went completely over Gabriel's head at times, hitting the mountain behind him. Michael knew this, understood this, and as such, knew exactly what to say.

"Imagine, Gabriel, that you were assigned a task that you felt was beneath you, that you did not want, nor ask for," Michael said. "And though I understand that you would do so, imagine if this task asked you to go against your friends? *Would you?* Or more importantly, why should you? Could you, of all of His angels, come up with your own plan to handle the situation?"

"I…" Gabriel frowned.

"And that is why some angels would disagree with His plan. Because they believe that they know best."

Just outside of the hall, a group of cherubims began a soft and melodic worship to Abba, Yeshua, and Eliezer. With harps complementing their voices, the two archangels stood silently for several moments, mesmerized by the beauty of the song.

And finally, Gabriel returned to the subject of their discussion. "But only He does," he said, dutifully and respectfully, and Michael had to hold back a wince. Gabriel was as sharp as his sword, Michael thought, but sadly, his focus on perfection could be his biggest detriment.

"However," Michael then responded, "that does not mean they cannot think for themselves. *That they can choose for themselves.* We are more than just tools, Gabriel. Abba knows this, and thus, allows this."

Gabriel gently shook his head. His loyalty and devotion, both virtues onto themselves, were now clashing against each other. "I…" his voice was uncertain, and his eyes were filled with confusion.

Michael winced, *had he pushed a bit too hard? No - it is a lesson better learned presently, no matter how difficult.* "Think of it this way," Michael said again, "let us imagine that you were ordered to maintain your position; but, you notice that, say, an enemy is carrying something important, what would you do?"

"Stay there, as I was ordered," Gabriel replied, confidently and without so much as a moment's pause.

"And, ask yourself … what do you believe Lucifer would do?"

Gabriel frowned. "He would…do *what he thinks is best.*"

"And just what would be best, given the circumstances? Confront the bearer of the item of importance, and thus leave his post, possibly allowing other dangerous forces to get through. *Do you see my point?*" Michael asked.

"Yes, sadly," Gabriel crossed his arms. For a moment, they felt the joy from Abba descending upon the cherubims outside the hall. The cherubims stopped their singing and broke out into joy-filled praises. Once this passed, Gabriel finished his thought. "I'm afraid that Lucifer is susceptible to these…rumors we have heard about. They seem to make him angry and yet, dare I say, jealous? It is much to consider, but I do admit that I feel obligated to make sure that he remains untainted. It is a very formidable concern which I carry."

Michael narrowed his eyes on Gabriel. "No, my friend. It means that Lucifer is able to decide his own course of action, and follow it through." Let us go out and journey now for a bit. Let us explore this great kingdom Abba has given us.

They left the hall and embarked on a casual float above the lower layers of First Heaven, watching the grandeur in all that was taking place by some of the three billion angels in this quadrant of the expansive kingdom. Worship events, songs, kneeling prayer devotionals, games of skill involving training with their new weaponry, relaxing in jovial laughter and discourse, *it seemed all was well* ….

Michael continued their conversation. "Like Lucifer, that is what many angels believe … that they are taking the correct course of action, though we might disagree with them as to what that action is, we cannot blame them for having such thoughts."

"And what if those actions go against Him?" Gabriel returned.

"Then we will do our best to bring them back," Michael said. "I trust you understand that I do not wish to suspect anyone, but…"

"You will do what you must, I understand," Gabriel nodded. Michael held back the huge sigh he felt building within his soul, and he had to pinch the bridge of his nose. Gabriel was akin to some… *cherubim who only wanted to love and smile, and find peace and comfort throughout all time.* Or perhaps some other creature Abba might one day create … one that was happy to stand guard and be with its owner. *Hmmm ….* Michael gave it further consideration. Yes, something perhaps which would walk on four legs…and be happy just to be with its master. *All the time.*

Making a mental note to propose such a glorious creation to Abba, if only because the idea of having a creature that was loyal and always happy would serve to validate the purpose of their very own creation. *Yes …* this appealed to Michael very much. With that thought, he smiled at Gabriel. "As for me, my friend. I will do what I need to."

"Yes, I know you will, *as if you have any other choice ….*" Gabriel said, smiling at his brother and shaking his head.

From beyond a cloud structure as magnificent as the Grand Hall itself, they suddenly saw Lucifer flying their way speedily.

"I do," Michael responded, "a small, but vital one. Much like how you would separate a greatsword from a longsword." Michael laughed at his own words.

"I do not follow, are they not both weapons?" Gabriel said. "Beyond the size and the shape, both achieve the same result."

Just as Lucifer approached and settled into a reclining position beside them, Michael shook his head and continued. "And the result is always the same - bloodshed, but, let me make it clear to you Gabriel, I will do my best to put these rumors to rest, and prevent any true conflict from breaking out."

"Seems I have arrived at an opportune moment in the dialogue," Lucifer said.

With a moment of relief washing over his face due to Michael's reassurance, Gabriel nodded at Lucifer.

"Yes, my friend," Michael said to Lucifer. "Gabriel has explained the occurrence earlier to me and we had been discussing any potential occasions which may arise."

"Do not worry, I have the means to keep my troops under control," Lucifer said.

Gabriel looked at Michael and tried to register his reaction, but Michael gave nothing away. "I know that," Michael said to Lucifer. "That was just what I had been telling Gabriel, however, he has deeper concerns about all being well."

Lucifer glanced at Gabriel and detected in his expression the hesitancy to his faith regarding all that was to come. "What is it, my brother? It is not like you to be so... *uncertain.*"

"I...I just cannot understand it," Gabriel muttered, and cast his gaze downwards. Gabriel himself felt as if he had just committed a shameful act in front of the Father, and was little more than newly created.

"That there would be discontent?" Lucifer asked.

"That there are those who would act against Him," Gabriel continued. "Do they not understand that He loves us? That He has provided all of First Heaven just for us?"

"I am sure that they do," Michael interjected. "But sometimes, *love is not enough.*"

"It should be," Gabriel countered. "What else is there but love? Love for your friends and brothers, love for the Elohim - *is that not what our very creation is all about?"*

Michael nodded, but clasped his hands behind his back.

Lucifer struggled to find something to say to ease Gabriel's mind.

"I trust you are not going to let this go," Michael said.

"I...cannot," Gabriel shook his head. "I wish to believe you Michael, I truly do, but I cannot help but fear the worst ...."

"You believe that there will be true conflict?" Lucifer asked. When Gabriel did not answer, his brows raised and he went on. *"That angels will want independence?"* And then he went one step further. *"That they will find the courage to display true disloyalty and rage?"*

The three gazed down at the busy legions of angels in the layers below. Silence filled the space between them and each was afraid of responding to Lucifer's questions.

Finally, Gabriel spoke, and his words came from a place deep within each of their souls. "I pray that I am wrong - they aim to betray us...."

Chapter Four

Perfection was, quite simply put, a problem. His Angels, His sons, born and bred to be perfect, to be flawless, were now becoming rather problematic.

Free will .... Abba frowned, and for a split second, questioned Himself. He was, after all, quite ... *new at this*. Making something out of nothing, making something grand ... was never an easy task. He understood this well, or, at least, He liked to think He did. Abba was all powerful, all knowing ... perfect.

My creations will strive for perfection, but will have many obstacles along the way towards that fulfillment. It will take their faith in Me to find it. Like it or not, they must work to find their own perfection by overcoming everything else.

And yet, He believed that his angels could get there, and foresaw that most of them would. And now, He was starting to have another idea for the creations to come. *What was perfection, truly? Was it the lack of any flaws, or was it overcoming those flaws?*

Would his chosen sons, Lucifer, Gabriel, and Michael, each be able to overcome theirs? He knew that was not what was to come, although part of Him hoped they would each have the willpower to see beyond themselves.

Cunning Lucifer ... he longed for freedom, to speak clearly, and be heard. Stalwart Gabriel, always so ready to defend others, but sometimes overstepping and unable to see what didn't need defending. Kind Michael, always willing to negotiate, but always so ready for battle.

They were perfect, each in their own ways, and yet, they were flawed. The test ahead would perfect them through trial by fire, or break them. The angels, as He made them, came equipped to achieve perfection, and yet would have to overcome pain and loss to do so. To grow, to struggle, to overcome, to succeed, was what Abba had intended for them in order to achieve their ends. *Thus the angels, as they were, had been born perfect.*

And thus, the predictable end of what was to come. *One angel would hit a hurdle they could not overcome with cunning, with strength, or with kindness,* and this made Abba terribly heart-broken. This angel would become a failure, and Abba, having given free will, was powerless to stop it. With too much drive, the understanding and the necessary learning to become more and overcome would not be enough. It will thus, *trap this angel in failure for all eternity.*

His vision always encompassed more. He had foreseen from the beginning of all time, *something that would grow, fail, cry, pick themselves back up, and try once again.* Something that would continue on, despite not being perfect, nor perhaps ever being perfected, but having the desire to achieve perfection nonetheless. *Flawed, but faithful.* And even more than that. His angels never had a choice in loving Him, never knew another life. This creation would know other faiths, other loves, other temptations. And when they chose to follow Him, then it would be their choice, not simply His own urging.

This creation would be flawed, imperfect, and oh so wonderful in all these things. They would multiply on their own, and be responsible for the care of new souls. They would have great capacities, but also great fallibilities. Abba contemplated, and waited for the total fruition of His idea to come together.

Then, the door between First and Second Heaven opened, and a familiar figure stood across the threshold. He stood tall, proud, and held a deep frown on his face. Lucifer had arrived, just as Abba had foreseen that he might.

"My Lord," he kneeled. "I come with ill news."

"And what might that be, my son?" Abba asked.

"Some of the angels are…how can I say it…are…"

"Discontent with their lot in life?" Abba asked.

With a jolt of sudden surprise flooding his system, Lucifer nodded. "Yes," he risked a glance upward, but as always, Abba's face was hidden by the familiar brilliant light. "How did you...."

"I am old, my son, not blind, nor deaf," Abba replied, and risked a coy smile. "Remember, I have already foreseen all that will come."

Lucifer stood. "Then, what do you plan to do?"

Abba knew His plans for all He created and would create. And He understood the longing that each soul would feel. Yet, how to say this kindly and without offending, that there would be a new creation to come? One flawed, imperfect, but ready to grow?

"I plan," Abba looked at Lucifer with a father's love. "To create something new in due time."

"Something new?" Lucifer blinked in surprise.

"Yes, there will be new worlds, you see. And as such, I believe there should be new creations to populate them."

"I...understand," Lucifer said, but his frown betrayed his disappointment. "But, what of us?"

"Of the angels? You will remain by my side, of course," Abba nodded. "Let that never be in doubt."

"But ...," Lucifer struggled to find words to adequately express this sudden and new inner turmoil felt deep inside. "Are we not enough?" he finally asked, and Abba frowned. *What Lucifer is really asking Me is: am I not enough?*

Silence descended between them as each considered their positions. Lucifer felt himself a cunning, capable, and fine commander. In the days to come, he would no doubt lead the charge against many enemies, *but right now?* He knew he needed to temper the growing disappointment which had begun piercing his heart. Somehow, Abba's words gave rise to his ego and pride feeling tarnished and waning.

Of course, Abba knew all too well the danger afoot when they let their ego and their pride drive their actions. He watched Lucifer closely.

"You are more than enough," Abba replied. "But that doesn't mean there can't be more. *More souls to love and to find my love.* Together in eternity, tested and true."

Abba sat back on His throne and Lucifer then leaned casually against a magnificent ivory pillar, his right leg bent with his foot against the pillar, and now letting his gaze depart from the bright glow of Abba to settle downwards, finally focusing on some angels in a green field practicing with their weapons and shields.

Abba continued. "Lucifer, I would have thought by now that you would have realized it is *the very battle between good and evil* that drives My purpose. *As it has for all time."* Abba paused and Lucifer felt surprised at His directness. "Each refined and tested soul glorifies Me and honors My very existence and purpose."

Lucifer considered this for a moment, but he could not help himself. *"But, more of what?"* he finally asked, betraying his mild dissatisfaction.

"More…life, *in my own image."* Abba paused to let it register. "More than armies of worshippers and soldiers …."

"You wish for, what precisely?" Lucifer stood up straight, finally allowing the anger inside to give way to uncharted, and quite possibly foolhardy, courage. "More worshippers? Slaves … workers?"

It said something about Lucifer's mindset that the first thing that came to his mind was 'labor.' *But, that was the way his mind was supposed to work, was it not?* Lucifer was cunning, no doubt, but that left a nasty habit of categorization as well. He knew his best worshippers well enough. And those who could fight became sorted and organized in his head. It was his way of keeping track of who could best perform when he needed them to.

But those who did not, would not, or could not fight became something else. And if they were not very good at worshiping and enduring the necessary repetition of such an act, then manual labor was the only thing left for him to value when it came to those within his army. He was an angel who tried seeing all the degrees of strength within others, and yet, many times he had been reminded by Gabriel and Michael that weakness itself could be a very important strength.

"No," Abba finally answered, his voice firm. "Something new, Lucifer. Something quite beyond what you see now."

"Beyond?" Lucifer repeated, and his face twisted into a scowl. "You speak as if there is something greater than an angel, something perhaps *even greater than You."*

But Abba knew that what Lucifer truly meant was much more concerning to the archangel: *something greater than me.*

Lucifer and his pride, such a deadly sin.

"What do you even intend to create?" Lucifer asked, his tone edging on a demand.

Abba waited for several moments before answering. "Something with less strength than the angels ... something which can understand pain and loss, and who will eventually realize that dependence upon me is the only thing that will save them *from their own destructive impulses.* Something... I will call *a human."*

"A what?" Lucifer asked, raising his brow.

"Lucifer, my son, please understand the fullness of my intentions. *I have no desire to replace you,* or to change you, but you must know that I have discovered a flaw." Abba did not want Lucifer to blame himself or the other angels. He continued, "This is my fault."

Surprised by this statement from Abba, Lucifer responded, "I, and any other angels, have been made according to your design. How can there possibly be a flaw?"

"Because I made you perfect," Abba returned. "You see, a perfect being cannot grow and cannot change." He saw that Lucifer did not yet understand. A longer period of silence followed, until eventually, Abba changed the immediate subject matter at hand. "Tell me, are you always going to be set in your ways?"

"As long as I need to," Lucifer returned.

"And how long is that?" Abba countered, to which Lucifer fell silent once again. After a moment, Abba spoke once more. "You see, that is my point exactly! Lucifer, I love you and I'll always love you.

Think about it, do you want solely angels, along with myself, to be the only creatures in existence when this trial is done?"

"Would that be so bad?" Lucifer asked.

"Not so bad, but it would be a mistake," Abba returned. "Think about it. If it was just us, the cosmos would be empty, filled only to a small dot for all the entirety of creation. What of the rest? Would you just let it sit as it gathers space dust?"

"I would, and plan to, find a use for it," Lucifer said.

"And would that use be for good, or for evil, for peace, or for war?" Abba asked, and Lucifer frowned.

"My Father, I mean no disrespect, but this…," Lucifer turned around to face the bright glow of Abba's countenance once again. "This sounds like you're replacing us. Replacing *me*. What would you say to Gabriel, to Michael? What of the Cherubs and the Seraphim? Have you not asked them what to make of this matter? Surely you, of all beings, can make more angels."

"And then what? Would I make only angels?" Abba raised a brow. "I have concluded that using only one stratagem will lead to failure, sooner or later."

"We are not speaking of the same thing!" Lucifer snapped, and then immediately recoiled as if he had been yanked backwards by a rope. And yet, with such a display of his anger towards Abba, Lucifer may as well have walked up to Abba and slapped him across the face.

Abba said nothing, and only contemplated the reaction of his archangel in charge of worship a bit further. As for himself, Lucifer cast his gaze to the floor, and he worked his jaw to no avail. What was there to say? *What was there to do?*

"I am…sorry, my Father," Lucifer grumbled. "I am speaking out of turn."

"See that you remember that this is a place of peace, not of arguments," Abba returned. "I have encouraged you to share your thoughts with me, and of course, those thoughts are not mine, *but yours."*

"I will," Lucifer said, and for a moment, Abba wanted to believe that was the case.

"Tell me something Lucifer," Abba began, "why do you loathe the idea so much?"

"I…" Lucifer attempted to choose his words very carefully. "I believe that we are all that you need."

***

Asher was good at many things, he was, after all, a child of Abba, and while he was not on the same plateau as the likes of Michael and Gabriel happily stood upon, he allowed himself a small measure of pride in that he was the kind of angel who could adjust to any circumstance.

But as of this moment, that 'ability' was being sorely tested.

He had heard rumors, whispers, talks among his brothers about Abba and Lucifer, that the former was a fool, an old man losing his touch and becoming something less than what they needed. Lies, all of it, but it didn't change the fact that more than a few angels had started engaging in more and more of these…well, Asher hesianted to truly call them 'discussions.'

And one such 'discussion' took place in front of him, led by that fool Zared. Asher remained perched above them, well out of sight by resting on an outcropping of rocks on a secluded part near the Remulon Garden. He watched and listened, and held himself back as Zared began to speak.

"Brothers," Zared said, "I'm sure that many of you are well aware, but these are troubling times. Weapons, armor … we are soldiers, the only question is, what do we do when we are done fighting?"

Another angel, one that Asher did not recognize, nodded in agreement. "We are not farmers," he said. "Not peasants, or lowly workers."

"My point exactly," Zared agreed.

"But then," another angel asked, his voice hesitant. "What if Abba knows? *He must.*"

"If He knows," Zared replied, "then it does not matter. If He had the will or the power to stop these discussions, which, I need to remind everyone, is all they are, then He would have done so by now."

"Are you certain?" Another one asked.

"Do you see any bolts of divine wrath coming down upon my head?" Zared returned, almost too confidently, and there was a moment when every angel in attendance, including Asher, waited for something to come and smite Zared down where he stood.

Nothing came, and he smiled.

Asher frowned, and shook his head. He fought back the urge to dive bomb them, to drop down and confront those who plotted against Abba.

But Asher did not raise a finger, for he was loyal, and like it or not, he knew that to truly expose these traitors, or dissenters if one wanted to be polite, *then he needed proof.*

Thankfully, Zared with his big and boastful mouth started talking again.

"Rest assured brothers," Zared said. "We are not alone, many of our kind have shared our doubts, our worries. From the lowest soldier to the highest commander, I believe that we can remain in this place that is rightfully ours." He paused, and Asher assumed he did it for dramatic purposes. *"Or better yet, take what is deserved,"* Zared exclaimed, clenching his fist.

Asher's jaw tightened and lines of concern furrowed across his brow.

"Brothers," Zared continued. "I speak now plainly and truthfully. Suffice to say, I am not the only one who believes that a change is in order."

"A change?" Asher muttered to himself.

"Though we are new, we are bound by laws we did not agree to, laws that bind us, tie us down, and chain us to the ground when we want nothing more than to soar freely through the clouds," Zared continued. "And the Archangels, those that keep us tied down with rules and commandments, are the ones who spread His will, His desires."

"What about us?" Another angel asked.

"Exactly," Zared nodded. *"What about us?* Do we not have a say in our destiny? Do we not have the right to choose where we fly? To go where we desire? We are perfect, is it not the right of a perfect species to take from those who might be imperfect?"

Asher frowned once more. Begrudgingly, he had once thought that Zared had been making good points. But now those points had been tossed out the window and hit the pillar on the way out, all to be replaced by this... *madness.*

"You speak of heresy," another angel said. *"You speak of going against Abba."*

"Yet, there is talk that He is planning to go against us! A new creation ... human. How will that all work out?" Zared returned. "And besides ... is it not the right of every son to break away from his Father? To become their own person?"

"But not with violence," the angel scorned. "You are coming much too close to a very thin line, Zared."

Zared scoffed. "I am a risk taker, as is my want. You cannot accomplish lasting change without the will to accept such risks."

"That risk," the angel replied, "is angering our Father."

"Then let him be angry," Zared returned. "Let him yell, let him command, but I, and I alone, will control my fate." He looked at the assembled group. "And I trust that goes for all of you, as well."

***

"Need and want are two very different things," Abba replied to Lucifer. "Not to say I do not enjoy your company, of course."

"Of course," Lucifer nodded. "But... *why must you?"*

"Because I have seen that there has been an error ... perhaps a miscalculation," Abba admitted. "I made you perfect, and in that perfection, for some of you, there is not enough ...."

"Enough what?"

"Fire burns, the wind blows, and the water falls from the rocks down into the pools below, these things are what they are, and cannot change. Neither can angels, I fear," Abba shook his head. "You are everlasting, but... for some of you, worshiping me is not enough all on its own. I am just now learning this lesson, Lucifer, and it disturbs me greatly."

"So, who is to blame then?" Lucifer wanted Abba to admit that this was His own wrongdoing. He wanted to feel justified that the grumblings and dissatisfactions of some angels amongst his troops was not his own fault. Finally, his anger bled through with no hope of stemming it. *"Why make something perfect if it is flawed?"* Lucifer growled, his previous tone forgotten.

"Perhaps, my son, the flaw is that love itself, instead of being seen correctly as the strength which drives all that is in existence, *somehow is viewed as weakness."* Abba turned and walked further into his chamber, each footstep falling softly against the golden metal floor. "And, as for you, Lucifer, what is your view on the power of My love?"

"Father, who am I to judge the value of your love? We all think of you as perfect, and you called us perfect." Yet, his anger flared once again as he thought about the polarity of his very nature and existence. Lucifer suddenly growled, *"Why did you say one thing, that we are perfect, and then tell me there are some whose behaviors contradict that?"*

"Because when I made you to be perfect," Abba returned. "I decided to give you free will. Some of you did not understand that perfection itself can be a flaw if it is not honored, or if it is taken for granted. *My son, cannot you not understand what I've been telling you?* What is perfect can only remain so if it chooses to be. If, in its singular state, it cannot find true happiness, it feels compelled to adapt and learn ways apart from Me and from My love. A truly perfect being knows that only through loyalty and dependence upon Me, can it always remain perfect, and nothing will ever change that."

"But—"

"And if that perfect being changes, and doesn't grow towards Me, is it then even truly alive? *Or is it dead?*"

"I do not—"

"Then please, understand that if you question, you are not perfect, that you are not ever going to be perfect again, nor are you always going to be the commander of my armies, of my angels."

Lucifer felt defeated. *Had he been given away by some angel? Was there even any recourse?*

Abba appealed to him. "Do you wish to be a perfect being, Lucifer? Do each and every one of your brothers?"

Lucifer nodded, but it was only half-hearted. His knees were on the floor and his arms were outstretched towards Abba, but he felt weakened and defeated.

Abba continued back to his throne, where He sat. When He spoke once again, each word that left His mouth hit Lucifer like a morning star to his skull, like a spear to the heart. "Because if you were truly, always, devoted to me in love, then you would not be questioning my new creation, Lucifer." Abba's voice was like iron, cold and powerful.

Lucifer frowned, and his nostrils flared. "Then...*it is as they say,* it is your fault because you made us flawed, and what is to come next? A new species full of imperfection and free will. *That will be a deadly combination, surely you can see that?*"

Abba frowned. "No, I will—"

But Lucifer turned on his heel, walked away, and then floated out into the air back down to First Heaven.

"I did not dismiss you," Abba called, and Lucifer said nothing in reply.

He didn't need to.

***

There was silence in the Remulon Garden, some angels took in Zared's words, others looked conflicted, but from Asher's distance, it was impossible to tell who would side with him, and who would side against him.

Then, Zared looked up and behind, directly at Asher. *"And what do you think?"*

Asher blinked once in surprise, and then slowly slinked backwards. *The idea that Zared had seen him was impossible, Asher was well above them, and hidden behind the outcropping of rocks, besides that.* Asher gave no notion he was even there, so how?

Then, the answer came.

Lucifer floated gently down, onto the crowd, and Asher's breath caught in his throat. *Lucifer, an archangel, was here?*

How? Why?

"My lord," Zared nodded in greeting. "So glad you could join us."

"Apologies for my being late. I…have had my own discussions now with Abba," Lucifer said, his gaze cast downward. "I no longer know with certainty that He has our best interests in His heart."

"Then, perhaps now, you can begin to listen to us instead?" Zared asked, and Lucifer nodded.

"I would be honored," Lucifer said, and crossed his arms, glancing upwards, right at Asher. "Though, perhaps our uninvited guest would care to join us, as well?"

Lucifer raised his hand, his spear forming into his grasp. With a frown, a surge of power ripped through the spear, firing off a beam right at Asher's hiding place.

Asher was many things, but he wasn't an Archangel. He dodged to the right, and while he was fast, he wasn't fast enough to avoid it entirely. It was only by a bit of luck that he managed to avoid the blast's direct center. *Perhaps, it had been that way by design.*

The rock he sat upon was burned through like paper, and his chest seared with pain as he fell forward towards the garden itself. Of course, falling was not new to Asher, nor to any angel who flew among the clouds, but this was certainly the first time he fell that was not under his direct control. In his pain, something he had never before felt, he was unable to regain command of his flight.

He landed with a meaty 'thunk' onto the grass, directly at the feet of Zared. His vision was blurry, and Asher blinked with the sudden realization that what he felt was quite distasteful. *This is...pain?*

He had been struck by a fellow angel, *by an archangel* ... Lucifer. His entire existence suddenly seemed to be worthless *and where was Abba when he needed Him? Or his own commander - Michael? What should he do next?*

"Well, Asher," Zared said, his tone all too pleased and self-righteous. Asher looked up into Zared's eyes and saw something he had never before witnessed. It was a combination of power and corruption, and it frightened him to his very core.

"How very kind of you to join us," Zared said, drawing his sword.

Chapter Five

Asher coughed, and noted that, by all intents and purposes, he was probably about to be a dead angel. "Zared," Asher growled.

"Asher," Zared returned, his tone calm, as if they had just bumped into each other in one of the halls.

"Why?" Asher spoke through a burning tongue. "Why do you speak so hatefully of our Father? Why do you rouse so many into anger?"

"Why?" Zared tilted his head. "Because anger is fire, brother. Fire spreads, its energy makes a greater heat, and puts events into motion. Without anger to fuel us, *can you really say that we are alive?*"

"Poetry does not disguise your words, Zared," Asher growled. *"You wish to rebel."*

At that, a moment of hesitation appeared in Zared's eyes. "I wish to be free," Zared said finally. "Free to make my own choices, wherever they may lead. I wish to do what I wish, and if someone opposes me? I wish for them to have the freedom to do so and then let the pieces fall where they may."

He kneeled down next to Asher.

"Might I grant you this very freedom that I sorely lack?" Zared asked, resting his sword on Asher's shoulder.

"I know not of where fallen angels may go," Asher growled. "But I shall grant you the freedom to fall there, if that is what you so strongly desire."

Zared smiled, "Well said, brother." With nothing more to say, Zared raised his sword, its blade gleaming in the brilliant and perpetual light of First Heaven. In that moment, an unfamiliar feeling welled up inside Asher. It felt cold, clammy even, and it rooted him to the spot as if the strongest of nature's vines had wrapped around his legs and fused together with them. His breath echoed in his ears as his heartbeat thundered ferociously. No matter how much he willed his legs to work, it was as if the message to move them could not get beyond his head. His body was frozen.

As Zared brought the blade down, a hand suddenly snapped upwards and caught Zared's arm in mid ark.

"Wait," Lucifer said. "Do not spill the blood of our family just yet, there is no cause for this."

"But my Lord," Zared replied. "He will besmirch us, call us rebels. Is it not better for him to be silenced?"

"He will...," Lucifer glanced down at Asher with an uncertain and somewhat distant look in his eyes. "Come around."

"He will?" Zared frowned.

"As your commanding officer, I order this meeting dispersed for now," he gestured towards Asher. "Take him somewhere safe. And Zared?"

Zared froze like his spine had been replaced with ice.

"We are not done," Lucifer said, his tone booking no argument. Zared nodded meekly, the wind taken out of his flight as he nodded. As the assembled angels left, save for two of Lucifer's guards who were beside Asher, Lucifer kneeled down in front of Asher. Looking into Asher's eyes, Lucifer shook his head. "We shall discuss this... later, but there is something you should know. Our Father intends to create another race, *one to replace us*. What you do with this knowledge is your choice, but I firmly suggest that you choose to use it wisely."

Asher nodded slowly, and finally was picked up off the ground by the arms of the two guardian angels.

Before long, he was carried away, up into the vast blue sky, *his legs still refusing to heed his mind's call to action.*

***

If there was one thing to say about Lucifer, it was thus: *he towered over almost all the other angels.* Perhaps it was to make him easier to spot on the battlefield, perhaps it was to instill a sense of deference among his soldiers. *Whatever the reason,* all that Zared knew as he kneeled before Lucifer was that the commander of the worshiping angels was one of the few who could instill true fear into others. As Lucifer stared down at the typically-sized, smaller angel, his gaze was unreadable, and his mouth curled into a stony frown. It was only the crackling of light shining through the upper portals of the hall which were illuminating the deep furrows across Lucifer's forehead, informing Zared that Lucifer was burning with anger under his otherwise calm visage.

"What were you thinking?" Lucifer asked in a polite tone - *but most certainly too polite,* where his tone was an actual mockery of Zared's judgment and behavior. Now it was Zared who felt like the victim, and in that moment, it seemed as if Lucifer had *transformed into another being altogether;* much different from who he had always been.

Nevertheless, he was unperturbed from stating his case. "That letting an enemy live was unwise," Zared returned.

"Asher is not our enemy! *He is our brother!"* Lucifer snapped. "Have you lost complete leave of your senses, soldier?"

"I am in full control," Zared said. "I know Asher well, he is stubborn ... foolish."

"That does not give you the right to attack him! To spill the blood of another angel is likened to destroying Abba's very own soul!" Lucifer frowned. "I allowed these talks to continue because I, too, have my doubts, *but we are not murderers* - not of our own kind!"

Zared dared to stand before Lucifer. "And what if we are? What if we knew we have the ability *to become more than we are presently?"*

"More?" Lucifer echoed. "You speak in riddles, and I order you to speak plainly."

"We deserve more, don't we? You've said this yourself." Zared rested his right hand upon his sheathed sword's handle. "*We are perfect,* my brother. Why should we serve with those who are content to be servants?"

At this, Lucifer growled. "Your words are as smooth as the glassy waters atop Rundon Pond, but your actions were pure savagery."

"I am what I am," Zared shook his head. "To be otherwise is a lie, and I am many things, *but I am not a liar.*"

"No, just a foolhardy actor on impulse who has decided to use his will for total freedom," Lucifer frowned, and then shook his head. "We will discuss this further, but as for now, there is to be an assembly. Abba has an announcement for us, although I suspect I already know what it will be."

"The truth finally to be revealed, which will verify all of these rumors we have attempted to counter for so long. You, too, do not seem *pleased*, my brother, *by what you know is to come.*" Zared said, an unfamiliar, challenging look in his eyes.

Lucifer snorted. *"Why should I be pleased?"* For a moment, he tried fighting against his own dissatisfaction, but it was pointless. Abba had not given him enough of the assurance he had craved to do so.

Staring into Zared's eyes, he felt weakened because he knew he could no longer promote complacency among a growing number of angels beneath his command. Hating to admit it, still, he had to hear his own thoughts out loud in the presence of one of his commanding officers once and for all. "This assembly will be our beloved Father's revelation that He is about to create *our replacements.*"

***

All would go very well, according to Abba's idea - after all, the angels were Bene-Elohim, sons of God, whose sole purpose was to love, honor, and respect Abba, Yeshua, and Eliezer, and to accept their places along with the of the Triune Elohim.

Before beginning the assembly, The Triune were meeting, just the three of them. Yeshua was discussing the various characteristics of the subordinate angels. "Some show weaknesses, and alliances, while others have strength in their allegiances to their archangels and to each other, while the strongest also align themselves well to the other archangels and their subordinates."

"However, with the length of days," Abba said, seeing that without purpose, some of the angels had become bored, "praising the Triune Elohim and receiving our love was not enough, and malice seeped into the minds of some. Boredom fed a need for isolation, for to be together in unity with us and with one another, the angels seemed to need a project."

"Yes, togetherness breeds competition," Yeshua said to Abba. "Whereas, boredom breeds contempt. Competition itself, if kept mild, gives rise to industry and a cooperative spirit intent on instilling the finest qualities amongst the majority. With a common goal, they do well and competition is meant only to instill productivity. Those who take competition too far are those whose weakness is their own vanity. Suffering dispels this illusion for the value of vanity."

Eliezer and Abba both nodded in agreement. "The fault, then," Abba said, "is where free will meets complacency and when boredom is thrown into this mix, they soon tend to believe in their own power and look after their own self-interests rather than what is best for all."

Now it was Yeshua who nodded. "It seems that without a common goal, the angels can become pesky."

"Or worse," Eliezer interjected. *"They appear to create conflict out of nothing.* Happiness in itself does not please them." His thoughts triggered a further reaction felt by Abba and Yeshua collectively, "And therefore, maybe happiness and love will never be enough to make some of them content."

"I have an answer for that, and such a purpose in mind," Abba responded.

As Yeshua and Eliezer had already known, Abba would create the Third Heaven, a place called earth, and with that, change would finally come. The angels' domain would thus become Second Heaven, while the Triune's home would become Third Heaven once and for all. And then Abba would create man ... *the perfect answer to all that was wrong with angels.*

"Come," Abba said. "Call the assembly to order."

***

The Grand Assembly was just as Gabriel had remembered it. Vast, impossibly wide, made possible only by the powers of Abba. Built vertically so the Angels may fly as high as they wished, or as low as they wanted. And yet, no matter how high or low they went, the voice of Abba reached them all as though he was standing directly beside them, guiding them.

Gabriel knew not of what Abba had to announce, but it seemed that Michael did, for as he joined Gabriel on a column overlooking the assembly, Michael immediately frowned.

"I have…concerns, as of late," Michael said.

"Allow me to speak plainly, brother," Gabriel said. "You are always concerned." It was a jest, not one of anger, or of mockery, but just a way to put Michael at ease.

It failed, and Michael said nothing more. Gabriel's mouth twitched downwards, and he cursed himself. He had no silver tongue when it came to casual conversation, nor ease of words, except for what messages spoken verbatim their Father wished for him to deliver. His strength lay with his abilities at gentle persuasion and to a somewhat lesser degree, his skills at arms.

Though, he rather wished the latter wasn't one of his better skills. He decided to take a tactful approach with Michael, seeing how deep in thought his fellow archangel was. "What do you believe our Father will announce?" Gabriel asked.

"I do not know…specifically," Michael said, and shook his head. "Forgive me Gabriel, I have been distracted as of late. Besides this assembly, an angel, Asher, has gone missing."

"Asher?" The name rang a bell, and Gabriel was able to put a face to it rather quickly. Asher had been the one to argue with that other one, Zared. "Are you certain?"

"Yes," Michael asked. "It is...strange. While it isn't impossible for one of us to become lost in the crowds, *at a time like this?* I made sure to double-check any and all angels in attendance."

Gabriel nodded and opened his mouth to speak ... only to fall silent *as a familiar voice spoke out.* He turned, and there, standing before all three billion of them, was Abba. Though the Grand Assembly Hall had no floor, that mattered little to the Maker.

"My children," Abba spoke. "My Angels, I come to make a proclamation." As Abba was speaking, twin lights descended, and Gabriel bowed his head, urged to do so by something deep within his soul. Yeshua and Eliezer suddenly appeared beside Abba, whose face was hidden behind a golden veil. His voice thundered tenderly as he continued. "I have made you our children and our worshipers, yet you are also fighters, soldiers, commanders, heroes ... and most of all, brothers. But, in that, I have realized my folly."

The words hit Gabriel like the bright, blazing, morning star. Their Father, Abba, had made a mistake? *That was impossible, incomprehensible.*

"I have *made* you; I did not give you a choice in the matter," Abba shook his head. "For this, in my ponderings, I have chosen to make a new purpose for all of us. A new heaven and a new embodiment of soul, one that can produce its own kind by choice. One that will be mortal, and not perfect by any means the way you are, but one that can choose to be perfect should they admit their own powerlessness and relinquish the free will I grant them *in order to devote their objectives and their dependency upon me.*"

Eliezer took up delivering the next part of the disclosure. His thoughts immediately filled each of the three billion minds below in first heaven. "They will be foolish, they will be, at times, nonsensical. They will give each of you an opportunity to harvest souls for their after life, once the embodiment of their spirit leaves this new first heaven behind."

Then Yeshua spoke next. "Nevertheless, I will ask that you welcome the new creation. Their lives will be filled with suffering if they do not choose the path Abba intends for them. They will be loved by each of us, nonetheless, and they are to be called Man ...."

Abba raised both his arms high in blessing. "In the beginning of the change that is soon to come, I shall create this new first heaven and call it *the earth*. And the earth will at first be without form, and void; and darkness will be upon the face of the deep. And Eliezer will move upon the face of the waters, wherefore, I shall proclaim, let there be light: and there shall be light. And upon seeing that the light was good: I shall divide the light from the darkness."

"And I shall call the light *Day*, and the darkness *Night*. And the evening and the morning will have taken place on the first day. And then I shall say, *let there be a firmament in the midst of the waters, and let it divide the waters from the waters*. And that is when I shall call the new firmament first heaven. And the evening and the morning would be the second day."

The angels were mostly in awe of what was to come, and they listened intently to Abba's voice and direction.

Abba continued, "I shall let the waters under the heaven be gathered together unto one place, and let the dry land appear. And that dry land is to be called the earth. And the gathering together of the waters shall be called the seas. It shall be good. I will then command the earth to bring forth grass, the herb yielding seed, and the fruit tree, yielding fruit after his kind, whose seed shall be in itself, upon the earth. This shall be done on the third day."

Michael had to remind himself that each day is considered by Abba to be an entire praise cycle worth three billion angelic devotions multiplied by the number of pages in the book of life itself. It was a number almost too huge to be considered or known. And Abba addressed this very thought of Michael's, saying, "There shall be lights in the firmament of this new first heaven to divide the day from the night; and let them be for signs, and for seasons, and for days, and years. Each cycle of day and night shall be considered one day by man."

Yeshua interjected, "And there shall be two lights in the firmament of this new heaven to give light upon the earth."

Eliezer completed Yeshua's thought by transmitting his thoughts to all souls. "Abba shall make two great lights; the greater light to rule the day, and the lesser light to rule the night. He shall make the stars appear in the firmament, also. And other worlds too numerous to count. This creation of the two lights will be on the fourth day."

He paused to take a watchful stare at the angels below. He was pleased to see many of them were growing more excited as He spoke. Abba continued, "The waters shall bring forth abundantly the moving creature that hath life, and fowl that may fly above the earth in the open firmament of heaven. And I shall then create great whales, and every living creature that moveth, which the waters brought forth abundantly, after their kind, and every winged fowl after his kind."

Yeshua and Eliezer looked across at all of the angels. Seeing that the vast majority were, to this point, taking this news so well, made them feel Abba was doing a good, *or even great,* thing for the benefit of all of them. Yeshua folded his arms across his chest in a bit of smug satisfaction, and He saw that it was all good.

Abba continued for a bit longer. "I shall bless them, and say such things to them like, be fruitful, and multiply, and fill the waters in the seas, and let fowl multiply in the earth. And the evening and the morning would then pass and that was to be *The Fifth Day*."

Many angels speculated about *when would it be the dawn of this new thing called man?* Abba knew their thoughts and now responded with, "I will then let the earth bring forth the living creature after his kind, cattle, and creeping thing, and beast of the earth after his kind. Everything which shall creepeth upon the earth will be able to bare future souls. It shall be good."

Then, there was a pause. A pause which lasted long enough for all three billion souls to know that the best announcement was about to come.

And then Abba announced, "We shall then make man in our image, after our likeness, out of the earth, and I shall breathe life into man: and let them have dominion over the fish of the sea, and over the fowl of the air, and over the cattle, and over all the earth, and over every creeping thing that creepeth upon the earth. But there shall also be created in our image, male *and female*, mind, body, and soul. The coupling of the male and female will cause the creation of new life, a new man, either male or female."

Abba lowered his hands and took ease. "And we shall bless them, and they shall worship the Elohim directly, without going through the angels. And neither shall the angels have dominion over man. We shall tell them to be fruitful, and multiply, and replenish the earth, and subdue it: and have dominion over the fish of the sea, and over the fowl of the air, and over every living thing that moveth upon the earth."

***

At first, the news was welcomed. A new species, man, to safeguard and protect. His angels were all too happy to have something to fight for, something they could grasp and safeguard: *a firm and manifest purpose.*

But not all of them. Among those angels who were unsettled with this news, what had previously been whispers, had become full blown rants; what had once been somewhat peaceful discussions, were now quickly becoming all-out arguments. There was a subtle change at first, which quickly turned into an entirely new atmosphere. No longer was their First Heaven so quiet, no longer as peaceful, and some would say, *no longer was it a just and kind place.* Lucifer understood this all too well, as Zared came bristling into his main hall.

"This is absurd!" Zared snapped. "We have served Him, and now, we are being replaced?! I knew it, *I knew it!"*

Lucifer frowned. "How nice to see you too, Zared," he said, his tone dry and burdened. "Please, come in, take a seat ... I am working on a new drink to help ease my pain. I believe I shall call it *Zared's silence*."

Zared frowned, shook his head, and then sat. Whether he liked it or not, Zared understood that Lucifer was not one to disrespect, if only because Lucifer could easily break his spine with the same ease one lifted a cup to drink. "I apologize, sir, but this is…"

"*Unacceptable?*" Lucifer raised a brow. "Yes, I agree. We were to be His servants, His heroes, but now, He is throwing us out because why? We have turned out to be not what He wanted?" Lucifer took a sip from his chalice. "Even His reasoning did not make any sense, as if He were making excuses for us." Lucifer paused to let his mind calculate what Abba had said at the conference. "Trust me, I understand the blame lies with Him and Him alone."

"Then, sir, we should protest this!" Zared exclaimed. "Do we not deserve the stations that we earned?"

Lucifer shook his head. "As much as I agree, I cannot make that happen. He can be…stubborn, as I have come to understand Him."

"Very true, Sir," Zared said, dismayed, his arms hanging at his side. "But, if that is the case, then what can we do?"

Lucifer frowned. "I am…working on it," he said, struggling to believe his own words. "There shall be a time soon to come when all will be right once again." And that was only a half lie, because he didn't know just how that would be so. "Tell me, what of your compatriots? Do they feel the same?"

"I have seen only a few," Zared said, "but I have the feeling that many others do not care for the humans the same way that most of our foolish brothers seem to."

Lucifer nodded. "Round up who you can, I wish to make a speech of my own."

Zared nodded. "And, if we encounter an angel who does not agree with us?"

At this, Lucifer hesitated. Though he disagreed with His father's – Abba's plan, the angels who agreed with Elohim bore none of His guilt, His mistake. To attack those angels would be tantamount to admitting that he was no better *than that fool of a father.* "No," Lucifer said. "Restrain yourselves as best you can, I do not wish to see any blood spilt upon these grounds."

"But if we are attacked, what then?" Zared demanded, and Lucifer was required to hold back a wince.

With his shoulders sagging and his head down, he said, *"Then do what you must."*

***

To say that the air was hot was an understatement, and he felt the tension had grown quite thick. To say that Joash did not have his doubts about this new First Heaven to come was like saying that Abba was unwise.

And Joash had his doubts, but he would never go so far....

This new First Heaven to be created by Abba as a home for this entirely new species called mankind, full of male and female humans ... *why?* Why did He feel this a necessity when Abba already had his angels beside Him? Were they simply not enough, or was the Father going off on a foolish tangent for some reason or other?

These questions, and many others, burned in Joash's thoughts, and as he walked through the halls to be in attendance for a meeting called by another angel, one named Zared, he found a familiar sight. Lucifer stood alone on a balcony, one that overlooked the clouds. For a moment, just a brief instant, Joash considered approaching him, asking him what to do next.

But that moment was fleeting and soon went away when a certain Midian came stomping right into his face. "What is this I hear?!" he snapped, and Joash had to admit, *an angry Midian was certainly new.* In all the time Joash had known him, he had pictured Midian to be the loyal sort, and had never imagined that he would experience what it would be like to receive his anger.

Only now, he didn't have to imagine it, for it was staring him right in the eye. "Hear what?" Joash asked, his voice calm.

"You - *these other angels,* are the rumors true? *That you wish to leave Abba's embrace?*"

If there were other angels who felt this way, Joash had to admit, he certainly understood their sentiments, and perhaps leaving Abba behind before they were all replaced by humans might be a viable option. He decided to act as if he knew more than he actually did. *"And if we are making such plans?"*

"Then you are a fool! Why would you wish to leave His warmth, His love, and His benevolence? To believe in some folly?"

"Because these thoughts which fester within me cannot be appeased. *Does Abba actually know His own mind?"* Joash returned. "I am not here to debate with you the finer qualities of my recrimination, but know this, if humans, or whatever they shall be called, are allowed to have free will, *then so am I."*

"Even when that means going against your very own nature, and doubting the wisdom of those who know better?" Midian asked, raising a brow.

Joash's knuckles tightened. *How dare he consider himself better than me?* He knew Midian well enough to know that the angel in front of him was as stubborn as they come. There could be no debate with Midian, no peaceful compromise, and no easy way out of this conversation right now. If he left now, then Midian would do two things: follow and badger him until the end of eternity; and disclose to Michael this very conversation.

Joash believed he was left with only one real option.

Without so much as a second thought, Joash pointedly glanced to the left, and Midian followed his gaze, just as he was hoping. This left Midian completely unprepared for Joashs's right hook, which immediately followed.

In a strange, almost perverse way, it felt very good to throw that punch, Joash thought. *Now, in the very least, regardless of what happened next, he had made his very own choice in how he had acted.*

Midian stumbled to his side, his senses ringing like the evening bell. "Y-you—*how dare you?"*

"You gave me no choice, Midian," Joash said. "To be honest, I grow weary of hearing you speak."

Midian's face twisted in pain, and not only from the blow struck to his head. He was shocked by this reaction from Joash, and he felt utterly unprepared for such extreme rejection. "You mean to say—"

"I am done speaking," Joash cut him off, cracking his knuckles. "And if you want to convince me of that *oh so grand plan Abba has in store for us,* then you'd best prepare to take action instead, brother."

Midian's face twisted into a snarl, and he realized words were getting him nowhere. He was enraged now that someone he had called *brother and friend* was suddenly an instant enemy. Without giving it a second thought, he launched himself right into Joash.

The two met in combat, fists flying with fury and fright, being unfamiliar against a former brother. Joash's anger guided him, his doubts leaving him with each fist thrown, every blow meeting its mark. But Midian's anger did not guide him; if anything, being so detested by his own soul, it hindered, and made his strikes sloppy, inaccurate.

For every swift, precise jab Joash delivered to Midian's midsection, he also wound up and threw a hefty haymaker that went sailing over Midian's head. However, it was in that anger wherein Joash found his resolve. As one punch finally found Midian's skull, it stirred something within Midian - a burning fire that soon erupted like a dying star.

Summoning all of his anger, all of his fury and spite, Midian let his arm fly, striking Joash in the ribs hard enough to leave an imprint of his fist.

Joash went flying backwards as the force of Midian's blow sent him against the opposite marble wall within the congregational hall, cracks spreading through it like a web, and Joash's vision went blank for a moment. He stumbled forward, took a shaky breath, and was utterly unprepared when Midian hurled himself directly at him once again. With this blast, the marble itself finally broke, and the two went flying through the wall and out into the garden.

They separated as they rolled onto the ground, pain rippling through both of their bodies. Faintly, the sound of voices reached their ears. Cries of concern, cries of anger, *and the clashing of weapons being drawn.*

Joash was pulled to his feet, not by his own power, but by that of another angel. Midian, however, rose alone, and soon angels friendly to him joined alongside him.

"What is the meaning of this?" Naphtali, one of the angels beside Midian, cried.

"Treason!" shouted Jael, Joash's companion angel who was standing directly behind Joash.

"No!" Joash laughed, "We are no traitors. After all, how can you be a traitor to a cause you no longer agree with?"

"You would go against your own Father?" Naphtali asked, for the first time realizing how serious the rebellion was.

"*He is not my father anymore,*" Joash chuckled. "And I am hardly a newly-created angel, unfamiliar with the routine and made to conform just for the sake of praising Him. From here, to the end of time, I alone shall decide my fate."

"*You—!*" Midian cried. Naphtali held him back from approaching any closer.

Jael stepped forward, his greataxe made of gold and silver on each blade, drawn. "I agree with Joash, I am no servant, *or tool!*"

"*You rebel against His plan?* He will make paradise!" Ammon, another angel close to Midian and Naphtali, stepped forward, his longsword at his side. "You would doom everyone just for your petty excuses?! You - being unable to conform because of your hurt pride? *Look at what you have reduced yourself to!*"

Joash looked at all of the gathered angels, the ones alongside and behind him, and the ones opposite him, standing with Midian and Naphtali. He then nodded at Ammon. "Better to burn in glowing embers with my pride *than to serve among the lost and weak within the clouds!*"

Suddenly, rage was renewed and all talking ceased. Glares across the schism and looks meant to kill were invoked. The feeling of the energy zapping between the two groups drained the component of innocence from the spirituality within First Heaven for the first time ever. Finally, violent intent erupted within their souls.

Ammon handed Midian his weapon, which had fallen to the ground during the brawl, and with that act, complete brutality broke out. The two sides collided in violence, and vengeance - brother fought brother.

Not one angel within the gathered crowd held back. Swords clashed against axes, lances against spears, fists slammed against bodies and shields. Techniques, and carefully refined practices, had no place in this brawl. In the heat of the rage felt - one side demanding their independence and free will, the other side holding the flame of love and devotion to Abba - it was soon an utter melee.

The two sides were barely able to distinguish friend from foe, and the battle lines changed and shifted with each passing moment. Angels fell to the ground, while others took the air to duel in the skies. Each holding to their firm conviction of being on the side which was the correct, just, and "right" cause.

Joash lost Midian in the fury, and as his heartbeat pounded with fury in his ears, he was almost deafened.

Combat rang through the halls, and sure enough, other angels were drawn to it. Some were confused, others flabbergasted at the sight of brothers brawling, but more than one took advantage of the confusion, and struck first the moment they identified the cause, and the reasons for combat.

And through it all, Lucifer watched, said nothing, did nothing. But as the brawl escalated, he smiled, hefted his spear, and steadily walked into the brawl. To the lesser angels, it was a chaotic mess, but to him, it was no less than a festive celebration. However, he knew his role well enough, and that heavenly eyes would see all and so he acted the part he had been created to achieve.

"Silence - *stop this behavior at once!*" Lucifer yelled, holding his spear above his head and aiming it towards whoever might challenge his authority.

Joash and Jael looked at Lucifer and were immediately disappointed. One side or the other, all battling ceased. Midian, Naphtali, and Ammon were surprised but momentarily grateful.

Lucifer nodded.

From within their thrones in Second Heaven, Abba turned to Yeshua and then to Eliezer. "The great schism is upon us. As we have foreseen for all eternity, *let it be done* …."

Chapter Six

The Elohim assembly was meeting with the three Archangels above the Jesuviah Garden. Abba on His throne in the middle with Yeshua on His right and Eliezer, a glowing spirit orb, to His left. In this meeting, the Elohim were telling the archangels They were about to create Earth, the stars, and the universe. And that soon, upon this earth, They will make a human out of the earth and breathe life first into man, and then from the man, create the female human called woman.

As He had already informed them during the general assembly earlier, Abba stated once again, that Man was then going to worship Elohim directly, and not be under the archangel's command.

Gabriel and Michael nodded, perched beneath the Elohim in prayerful repose among the grass and flowers. Lucifer sat up from his prone position to glance towards Elohim. "Yes, we know that already; as well, you have informed us that this "man" will be in the image of Elohim's mind, body, and soul. And that you are giving them free will …."

Gabriel and Michael were surprised at Lucifer's tone, and they glanced at him, peering into his countenance, his eyes, and his posture. Michael attempted to counter the tone he had used speaking so frankly to Abba. "I believe Lucifer is concerned, Abba, and he feels that mankind will have little use for angels or Elohim alike."

"We shall see," Abba responded immediately. "And that, in and of itself, is Divine Purpose. As for the angels, man will have use for you, *as will I have great use for you on their very behalf.*"

The archangels became curious and waited with high anticipation for Abba's next words. Lucifer relaxed back against the rock he had earlier been reclining upon. After a quick glance at their comrades, each of the archangels aligned their sights once again upon Abba.

Who then spoke with much authority and power. "As had always been intended, Michael and his army will be My warrior angels, ready to respond and intervene at My request when man has come to blows, or escalating conflict, and he will help to ensure My will intervenes, when I deem it appropriate, on earth and between man and his factions."

Yeshua sat up in his throne and marveled at the perfect creation that was Michael, in all of his glory. Michael nodded respectfully towards the Elohim and reposed once again, as Abba then continued.

"Gabriel, and his legions beneath his command, will be My messenger angels, ready to deliver My words and My thoughts to mankind, in an instant, as I see fit to intervene with some of the humans most deserving of My guidance and wisdom."

Gabriel sat up straight and felt honored to be such an important part of Elohim's newest creation. Glancing at Elohim, he felt Eliezer's love and might especially. Abba then finished with his last thoughts as He had intended to do before beginning the new creation.

"As for Lucifer, and all of his brothers beneath his command, the most important role of all: that of assisting mankind with their paramount duty and purpose while they are embodied on earth - *in their role worshiping Us.*"

Lucifer had feared hearing these very words, and he was ready and prepared to question Abba. *"But You, my Lord,* have already shared with me yourself, regarding the angels, there are some who will not succumb to giving You praise and love only, *even for You who deserve every bit of it.* If I may be so bold as to offer my concerns: *why do you believe these humans will be any different?"*

Abba stared at Lucifer, and Lucifer felt it; even if he could not see Abba's face directly. However, though He had acquired Abba's attention, *the Father of all remained silent.* Lucifer grew angrier the longer the pause accelerated in time and space. Until he could not stand the tension it created any further.

Why won't He answer me? He turned to see Michael and Gabriel with their perplexed looks gazing in his direction. Lucifer felt so very alone at that moment. Isolated, as if any question or concern coming from an archangel was a direct assault of the Father.

But it should not be so! Don't we have the right to challenge something which goes against nature itself? Humans will not be bred solely to worship, as the angels had been. He felt like he had to challenge Abba, since Abba seemed to be unaware of what this might do to the angels beneath his own command - his most pressing doubt and concern. "Heavenly Father, listen to me as I speak. I do thou listen to you always, for once hear my worry. *Even some of my own angels will not listen to me* - I cannot get them to respond in worship or to be full of praise for You any longer. How will I be able to do anything of the sort with man, who will not even be under my command?"

Michael and Gabriel felt like they should intervene, however, they dared not.

It was finally Yeshua who spoke. "Yes, Lucifer, as we well know. A leader ... *a commander,* teaches mostly by example. Sometimes he has to suffer through whatever it is his disciples undergo. His best students learn by watching his every gesture, how he endures suffering, how he inspires those beneath his command *to have faith and hope in Abba, alas, the entire Trinity of Elohim.*"

Yeshua stopped and again, there was a long pause.

Lucifer put his head down. "I do not ... understand what is required of me, then. I have tried, but the task is too big. *Free will makes us faulty, not perfect.* I need assistance if I am to get every single one of the angels back on track, worshipful and gracious, full of gratitude and not misery, and especially not questioning if there is anything better for themselves."

When He finally responded to Lucifer, His voice was full of compassion and understanding, and yet there was also a touch of reprimand. "Gabriel and Michael too, have some dissenters among their ranks, however, they have not gone to the extremes that yours have," Abba finally said.

This only served to enrage Lucifer the more. *"What are you saying...?"* Lucifer responded.

"It is just an observation, Lucifer," Eliezer transmitted to all present. "Please listen and think through your response."

"Am I to blame?" Lucifer asked.

"Each one is to decide for himself who is to blame and how free will acts upon groups and yet also within each individual," Yeshua responded. "Who is stronger - the one who succumbs to his friends' needs and desires, or the one who rises above the rest and provides a better example? Who gets his reward immediately, and who has to wait for their own recompense? Why then do some remain faithful while others flock together to find fault and misery?"

Eliezer transmitted a thought to all present. "Were Yeshua's words the help you desired from Us? If not, then perhaps Michael or Gabriel can add to the discussion and offer something in the way of salvation."

Before either of them could respond, Abba raised His right hand to silence them. "How long have you waited in secret with your own doubts?" Abba requested Lucifer.

He did not respond, for he did not know how to at this point.

And then Abba asked, "Will you, *they,* come around, or is there already too large an expanse between what is and what should be? Will it be Perdition or Salvation?"

"These are the only questions We can provide in the way of assistance at this place in time," Eliezer intervened. "If you cannot turn your own brothers back to Us, then what hope will there be for humans when We have assigned you the task of assisting them with their duties in worshiping Us?"

Lucifer felt dejected, scorned, and lost - as if he was being attacked by his very makers. He had no answer ... *yet.*

Meantime, Abba was ready for what was to come next. "Enough of this - as something requiring effort alone cannot be appeased with discussion."

He stood in all of His grandeur and said, "The hour has come." Raising his vast right hand, suddenly a new firmament appeared just beneath them, filling the nothingness and void that had been there forever. It was beautiful, majestic, endless, and serene; however, dark and cold at the very same time. It was the entire universe all in a flash. They all gazed in utter awe at its continuously growing mass.

Eliezer looked and saw that it was so. "It is good."

And then, with a wave of Abba's left hand, and then a shock of might from His right hand, planets, and stars too numerous to count filled the entire new universe. "Yes, and it shall be so," Abba said. "Finally, now the new First Heaven which is meant for the humans to come." He held out His right hand and with an intense thought, suddenly a spinning blue and green planet came into existence within the universe.

"Earth," Michael said.

Yeshua nodded.

Gazing down, they saw that all three billion angels were at the same time marveling at the newest creation from Abba.

Eliezer had a thought, which penetrated the archangels, and also each of the angel's souls in what was now Second Heaven, all at the same time. *"We are always here, and we love you, and you must remember that you were created just to enjoy the love we have for you. Now is the time - the moment has come for each to make their allegiances and their commitments. Yes, we hope to have your love for all time, as we will all mankind, once he is created. Like yours, their role will be to worship and to honor, love, and obey Abba, his son Yeshua, and me, Eliezer, who is the Spirit of love itself. Anything else will soon be met with isolation and misery, as you shall see."*

***

"Once I thought of myself as a friend, once I thought of myself as a brother. Once, I thought of myself as a son," Lucifer stepped forward. *"Once."*

Zared and Joash nodded in unison and said nothing as Lucifer continued to stride forward. They had met in a secluded spot, one they hoped was hidden even from Abba's eyes. It was no small feat, finding this little nook far out along the reaches of the vastness of what was now Second Heaven. Due to the questions of what was to come, Lucifer could do no less. For now, it seemed that for all his worry, his hesitation had finally left him, and now, Lucifer stood tall and proud as he continued to speak.

"We served Him, fought for Him, *bled* for Him, and what does He do? Blame us for his mistakes, his failures, and then think He's to try again? *For what?* Another species that will mindlessly worship Him? I must now admit to my true brothers that I am quite upset that I did not see this sooner!"

Lucifer turned. "What a fool I was, but a fool no longer. Abba, damn his name, is trying to foster his mistakes on a new species, a blind species that will be created as weak and as weary as a cloud on high. No, my brothers, my *true* kin, we must not let this happen. For we have *taken* free will for ourselves, and we *will* make our choices. For good, or for ill, for damnation or salvation, I am *done* being His servant, His tool. My name is Lucifer, and do I stand alone?"

Before him, an assembled crowd of angels stood in attention, each one cheering him on, repeating his name in a devilish chant. "LUCI-FER! *LUCI-FER!*"

Lucifer nodded, a swell of something that could only be called pride festering within him. *Is this what it is like to be worshiped? To be at the top?*

If so, he certainly didn't hate it.

If anything, he could certainly get used to it.

A touch to his shoulder caught his attention, and Lucifer turned to find Zared standing before him. "What is it?" he asked.

"The angel we captured, Asher, is there anything more you wish to gain from him?" Zared asked.

Lucifer thought for a moment. Asher was a loyal dog to that fool, Abba. Devout…but at the same time, a blind fool had its uses. An idea clicked in Lucifer's head. It was a simple one, but cunning. *Abba has used trickery on His foolish ones … and to beat him at his own game, I must undergo to become even more full of tricks and devious schemes.*

He considered his plan. *Yes, that could work, and all I need is to convince him of my inherent goodness - a simple spell to weave.*

"I will see him personally," Lucifer said.

"My lord?" Zared tilted his head. "What are you planning to do next? As angry as we are with Abba, we cannot hope to match his forces, or Him in a direct confrontation."

"Then we simply have to make up for what we lack in power in will and wits," Lucifer replied. "And I believe that our good friend Asher will be of great use to us. *Let us see how he feels about being free, shall we?*"

***

Gabriel was distraught. The recent turn of events regarding his friend Lucifer being bitter about the creation of this new species called man had felt like a blow to his gut. He wanted so badly to talk sense into Lucifer, but Michael had warned him that it was going to come to this - "A reckoning of angels each taking a side in the growing dispute and conflict," he had stated. As he thought about Michael's words, he considered they were a gross understatement by any measure.

Lucifer, his friend, his *brother* had committed one of the most heinous crimes in existence, he had taken one of his brothers into custody - keeping him bound by clasps against his own free will. *And for what? His own selfish, petty ego?*

Could it be that the Lucifer he knew back then was a lie? A mistake?

He held his chin in his right hand for a while, and then finally, he ran a hand through his hair. This was so surreal: a day, a week, a month ago, everything was in its place, the way it should have been. They had just gotten new armor, new weapons, all to wage a war of peace in His name, to spread devotion and love for Abba, and for the entire Elohim, throughout any new worlds to come. Most angels knew that Abba's desire was simply to create something better.

Now, it looked like Gabriel and his legions, along with Michael and his, were going to fight against their own brothers. *How could this have come to pass? I don't understand it and I don't like it.* But for Abba's sake, he had little doubt that he would fight. *I am going to have to fight against Lucifer.*

Gabriel, despite what others said about him, wasn't as stalwart as they wanted to believe. Like anyone else, he had his doubts, his worries, and concerns. The simple fact of the matter was that he wasn't like his brothers in one simple way. He understood that, at the end of it all, it wasn't about him, and thus, he pushed whatever fears he had to the wayside, and struggled onwards.

But even so, these recent events - Lucifer's betrayal of the heart, the war in the halls, and now this new species he was tasked to safeguard - even for him, it was a lot.

And as he walked, or rather, trudged into Michael's main meeting hall once more, Gabriel's shoulders slumped with a weight he did not ask for, but carried, nevertheless.

Michael was, as always, hard at work, going over the latest reports. However, this time, a rather unexpected change: his expression oozed anger. Gabriel hoped it was due to stress rather than hate.

"Gabriel," Michael said without looking up.

"Michael," Gabriel returned. "You look heavy."

"I think light would be the better word," Michael replied, "I haven't been eating as much of the manna as I would customarily."

"Do we even need to eat it, or anything else, for that matter?"

"I do not know with certainty," Michael said. "Nonetheless, it is a great boost for me when I do partake. Safe to say, for now, I miss the taste of it …."

"Abba knows. He will provide you with what is necessary."

"Yes, I know He will. Though, He has been rather busy lately …."

"I am sure it will come soon enough." Even though this was a simple topic and enjoyable to discuss, Gabriel realized that it was not the important one they needed to voice.

With an unfamiliar ache in his throat, Gabriel swallowed his fear. "Lucifer has…"

Michael shook his head. "I know; that damn fool."

Despite himself, despite all that he had seen and done, Gabriel still found it in him to respond with surprise. *"Michael?"*

Michael knew what he was going to ask, but instead of responding to Gabriel with an inquisitive *yes*, he responded by addressing the frustrations within his very own soul. "We were meant to be more," Michael said, his voice laden with despondency. "Not to be just soldiers, not to be just fighters. We were meant to be perfect in our worship and praise to Abba, but we were also meant to find out for ourselves just who we are." He turned to see Gabriel taking in his every word. "But we were not meant to harm another … *not to harm another brother,* Gabriel, no matter what. However, I fear we are to become a mighty army in need of defending the Kingdom of God."

He raised his head, and part of Gabriel's soul united with Michael's at that very moment. Down Michael's cheeks were the stains of tears. Not the kind that came from a gentle cry, but a true breakdown. "Where do we go wrong, Gabriel?"

He searched his mind for answers and found none. He searched his soul for replies and found it silent. All Gabriel could do was hang his head, and mutter. "I don't know," he said. "I thought all was well, how could we all have been so blind?"

"It's not your fault," Michael said on reflection alone. "I believe Abba, Yeshua, and Eliezer have foreseen all of what is to come for all eternity. They have prepared us all along the way, we just did not understand the scope of our mission until now."

But perhaps it was Gabriel's fault, as it was Michael's. Deep within, they both felt the same thing: *it could be they had been so wrapped up in their own personal thoughts that they neglected to notice the pain felt so severely by one of their brothers.*

"Is…is there nothing we can do to bring him back?" Gabriel asked.

"I don't know," Michael said, his face set rigidly, like a statue about to crack from the strain. Then he shook his head and fire blazed out of his eyes as he addressed Gabriel once again. "Lucifer is too far gone; our brother is forever lost…."

"I'm not giving up on him, not yet," Gabriel returned.

***

His spear twirled in his hands, and it found its mark with ease. Those angels - the ones who stood against his cause, fell to his razor-sharp blade, which easily found the weakness in their armor. He felt like a painter creating new artwork. Though none of his blows were fatal, none were kind either. Those who finally noticed that Archangel Lucifer himself had joined the fight, tried to defend Abba against the traitor, but Lucifer's dancing spear work was too much for them to overcome, and none of them had what it took.

One by one, the angels who stayed loyal to Abba fell to Lucifer's spear, and he smiled.

At last, he was free.

A small touch at his side took him from his imagination and informed him to stop burying himself in his thoughts and fantasies, time to get back to work. From here on out, he was a rebel, a traitor, and that meant he would have put in the extra hours.

He glanced to his left to see who had reached out for him, and found Zared at his side, breathing heavily and panting, a freshly used sword and shield at his side. "S-sir," he said, "have you finally decided to join us, *fully?*"

Lucifer nodded, "I have."

"Then, what should we do?" Zared asked, and Lucifer took a precious moment to curse Abba once more. While he stood as one of the greatest Angels in Heaven, the lesser of his kin had yet to prove themselves as fast a thinker as he was. That was fine on its own, but costly in the middle of a battle. He pointed northward.

They stood in the middle of the Second Heaven, and they needed to get out, now. No longer could they hide in shadows, no longer could they talk in whispers. No, for the rebels, they needed to escape. The only problem with that was there was an army between them and the exit, and there wasn't a clean way out. No tricks or cunning plans would suffice, only force and fury would see them through.

Of course, it also meant that it was a good way to show to Abba that his loyal angels were not invincible - a plus in Lucifer's mind. In that moment, a plan began to culminate within Lucifer's thoughts.

But at the moment, things were, quite naturally, a bit of a mess. While brute force was the only option available to him, it quickly dawned on Lucifer that having each of his angels created with their own free will was a noble quality unto itself: it made cohesion, discipline, and formation a thing of the past. Each of his rebels fought by themselves, for themselves, and knew next to nothing about covering another's back. Granted, those who were friends tried to work with their kin, but for the most part, they fought by themselves. *How to turn that into an asset?* With the wheels of his cunning moving at light speed, Lucifer fomented a plan that seemed most likely to bring victory.

Which is why I need my best fliers to handle something very important. Finally answering Zared's question, he turned to his commanding officer and said, "Take who you can, Zared, the best flyers, *and rip the pearly gate from its hinges!"*

That gate was the large, complicated, castle-like structure made out of divine pearls - a brilliant white, sturdy, and beautiful, with two huge columns extending from the base all the way to the highest reaches of the heavens. *It had always separated the angels' kingdom from the Elohim's.* There was nothing in their arsenal that could break through it, not Lucifer's spear, nor any of Zared's weapons.

Of course, that only applied to the gate itself, its interior workings, on the other hand.... Well, that was much, much easier to break.

Zared nodded, motioned to a nearby group of angels to follow, and took to the air.

This, in turn, left Lucifer alone with his own, private, objective in mind. Abba was certainly watching, or at the very least, going to watch at some point. He didn't know how often Abba, Yeshua, or Eliezer watched him, and come to think of it, the old fool never told Lucifer anything about what he wanted to know. But that was fine, because now, *Lucifer had a few things to tell him.* And he was not about to hold back!

Lucifer checked his thoughts, and for a brief moment, he was of two minds - thinking that somehow when he was angered, his words and thoughts could become so...juvenile. Blaming it on his newly acquired and earned freedom, he took to the sky.

Below him, the battles between the angels loyal to Abba versus the angels loyal only to their own freedom began erupting throughout many distinct quadrants of Second Heaven.

Lucifer watched one or two of them, happy to see they were going in his direction: *for now, at least.* While the chaotic mess he was leaving behind would falter without a leader guiding them in every moment, they could hold their own for a while as Lucifer took care of one item on his agenda. He understood what he had to do to make it official. He then told those loyal to his side that once that gate came down, they would know what to do.

In the meantime, it was time to have a talk with his dear old father ....

Chapter Seven

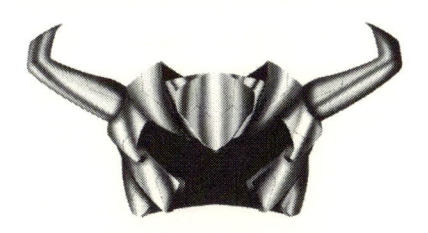

Let it never be said that Abba was hard to find, or hard to approach, despite being God. Zared and his men had done their job well, and Lucifer sailed right through the fallen gates. Once he had made it through the pearly gates of Third Heaven, it was easy to traverse the barren space until he reached God's kingdom itself. No guards awaited outside of his throne room, no warnings had been triggered, and it seemed as if there was absolutely no security. For anyone else, it would be foolish.

For Abba, it was unnecessary. Lucifer, at the very least, could appreciate that, and for that appreciation, it was why he chose to simply push the doors aside instead of knocking them down. They were, after all, very nice doors made of ivory and marble, gold and silver infused throughout. It would be a shame to ruin them. Still, something about them seemed…off. False, even. But he cast the thought aside and moved forward. If Abba was capable of trickery, then surely Lucifer would know.

"Where are you going?" Lucifer heard the words and turned to his left to find one of Michael's commanders staring at him, his sword poised and ready to strike.

Lucifer glared at him with fire in his eyes. "Don't stop me now, Petrovus! I am in no mood for delay. I have important business with Abba, and I mean to keep it."

"I know your intentions, Lucifer," Petrovus said. "If you mean to see Abba under these terms, then for your own good I mean to stop you." Petrovus took a step in front of Lucifer, who knew immediately he was going to fail this test of Michael's miserably.

Standing stoically, Lucifer said, "I am giving you this one warning and then you shall see a side of Lucifer you have never before witnessed. Step away from my path and do not intervene. Move this moment, or this action you have taken to try stopping my mission will be all you will ever do with the rest of your miserable life!"

"Turn now, Lucifer! *Or this decision you will make* will be the very last thing you will have ever done while living beneath the grace of our dear Lord Abba. Your fate will become the fate of all who follow you, and also the same for all the humans who fail to follow Abba. And it shall never be undone. Your decision now will last for all eternity. That is all I will say. Stop now!" With that Petrovus lowered his sword to his side and then took a step towards Lucifer with his right hand raised. "C'mon, turn and follow me," Petrovus said, meaning to put his right hand on Lucifer's shoulder to encourage him to turn around.

Raising his spear, he darted at Petrovus, who immediately engaged his sword and slung it up towards Lucifer's heart. Lucifer quickly dodged the blade, ducked and turned, then came back with a jab of his spear right into Petrovus's neck. It happened all too quickly and Petrovus had never prepared for such a sudden attack by Lucifer. He took a few steps backwards, and then grabbed at his neck with his hand, dropping his sword. Realizing he was severely wounded, he fell to his knees and then collapsed altogether.

With no other obstacle or angel in sight, Lucifer strode onwards until he arrived at Abba's temple room. He immediately taught himself how to not bother to think about such a trivial thing as having shed the blood of another angel. *Other matters at hand were more pressing - such as right now addressing all that Abba had done against every single one of the angels - abandoning them in favor of humans.* He tried to ignore the sound of his own vibrating heartbeat ringing in his ears. The burning in his throat was bad enough, but nevertheless, he pressed on.

Let it never be said that Lucifer was a coward.

He found Abba, sitting behind a grand desk which was magnificent in its size and design, and Lucifer noted that gold seemed to decorate so much of their inner kingdom. Every inch of it was covered in tomes, seals, and sturdy documents presented by the archangels which contained all of their ideas, reports, and more. The magnitude of all of the records would have been much too much for anyone else, but for Abba, it was necessary to keep some kind of record for all that passed by him each day.

"Father," Lucifer said.

"Son," Abba glanced at the spear in Lucifer's hand, still dripping red. "I see you've been arguing with your brothers."

"We've had quite a few disagreements as of late, I must admit," Lucifer said, and hefted the spear onto his shoulder. "Lately though, I've been wondering as to whether or not they are my brothers."

"As I am your Father as well as theirs, by definition I imagine they are," Abba said, his tone drier than the desert in second heaven that hadn't seen rain for a thousand years.

"Ah, but therein lies the paradox. If I am given free will, then am I not allowed to choose who my brothers are?" Lucifer returned. "I mean, you did the same, given that you *oh so graciously* chose to make an entirely new creation, instead of tending to the current one."

"You sound disappointed. That is—"

"And since we're on that subject," Lucifer cut Abba off. *"Let me broach with you another question,* one that's been haunting my mind for quite some time. Why are we soldiers?" Lucifer asked. "You are, with no embellishment whatsoever, the most powerful being in all creation *without any of us!* Why do you even need soldiers, warriors? *Why have you given us arms and armor?"* Lucifer frowned. "Don't tell me it's because you can't stand to hurt another, when you very easily gave us the tools to do so."

Abba frowned, and Lucifer smiled. It seemed that the conversation was going his way, as he had hoped.

Or, at least, that's what he thought until Abba lightly tapped the ground of Third Heaven once with his foot. Suddenly, all of the walls surrounding the room fell away.

Lucifer hefted his spear, ready to fight, as he realized that he had, in very simple terms, made a mistake.

Once all the walls had disappeared, he realized that he was actually in the throne room and there, suddenly Yeshua and Eliezer were seated on thrones beside Abba. Before him stood familiar faces, Michael, Gabriel, and also those who remained otherwise unfamiliar: *those useless cherubs, and that suck-up Seraphim.*

All loyal lapdogs of Abba.

"Lucifer," Gabriel said, his voice softer than Lucifer had ever heard it. "I have only one question for you, *why?*"

All eyes lay upon him, and despite everything, Lucifer found it in himself to chuckle.

"*Why?*" Lucifer smiled, and it was not a kind and welcoming smile, but something unGodly. "Why? Because I choose to," he said. He turned in a semi-circle to face each of his accusers, his spear jutting out at each of them, in turn. "If Abba has chosen to give us our own will like he has chosen to give it those *humans to come,*" he spat these words out like they were part of a grand curse on all of the living creations from Abba. "*Then I have the freedom to do with my will as I see fit.*"

"By harming your brothers?" Michael asked.

Lucifer shook his head. He was amazed at how confident he felt, despite having his back almost literally against the wall. Perhaps it was because he had nowhere to go now that anger had unleashed his spirit, or maybe it was because now, he finally understood why he hated being Abba's guardian after all.

As he stared into the eyes of his former brothers, a thought suddenly hit him like a rock flying out from within the bowels of heaven itself. *For all the talk about free will, for all of the bantering and worthless air that left their mouths, no one had free will, not really. Not so long as Abba drew breath and existed as the supreme entity.*

No - it was simple math. So long as Abba *existed*, Lucifer would never truly know peace, nor would he ever enjoy any kind of freedom. *After all, how can one be free, if there was one who planned for everything? Free will itself is therefore a contradiction, a paradox, if ever I heard one. Abba must go!*

As if reading his thoughts, Gabriel asked, "Tell me something. What is it that you hold onto so firmly which makes you believe you have the right to spill blood so readily? Abba has shown us your plans, your thoughts. Why must you feel it is your duty to prolong this rebellion, started by angels beneath your charge - *the very ones who not long ago you had complained to all of us about?*"

"You speak as though I had any choice, and as if we have already lost," Lucifer said. Resting his spear on his shoulder, he let out a hollow chuckle which resonated and echoed throughout the halls of the throne room. "Who knows? Maybe we have all lost, and we just haven't realized it."

"You must know that you can't win," Michael said, his piercing blue eyes shooting daggers at Lucifer. "No matter what tricks you may use to convince others of your righteous cause, no matter what banners you may use to rally those beneath your command, you will fail in all of your designs."

"How can you be so sure?" Lucifer answered. "However it may be that I win or lose is yet to be seen. And even so, perhaps even though we do not win, we can make certain that by our efforts for all time to come, *we do not lose.*"

Gabriel shook his head and put his hand upon his own weapon. "Are you truly so set on this vengeful course? All just meant that it may satiate your damaged, self-centered, and gluttoness pride?"

He chuckled once again. "All to save myself from a fate that I did not agree to," Lucifer returned. "All to save myself from a cause I could no longer support, and in fact, never had desired. Now, you blame me for having started a rebellion and tell me that nobody could see it was coming all along, when none of you had offered to help me to quell its fire. *Was I to be taken as a fool, Gabriel?*"

Lucifer was of the strong belief that his own words were true, unabashed, and to him, a simple statement of fact that none could dispute. But to Gabriel, he found within those very words a strong plea, and a call to salvage what remained of their once strong friendship.

"Then come back!" With a leap of utter desperation, Gabriel landed in front of Lucifer, his greatsword resting on his back. *"Lucifer, brother, there's still time to come back to us, to come back to the light."*

All eyes focused exclusively upon him; Lucifer smiled so despicably until his very jowls seemed to detach from his jaw. He reached out, gently, kindly, and placed his hand on Gabriel's shoulder, at the same time noticing that Gabriel's neck was unguarded.

"My brother, my once dear friend," Lucifer said, "It is far better to rule my own suffering than to serve someone else's idea of *paradise*. Perhaps when I succeed, I will take you with me as we rise above Abba's own throne to be exalted by all of the angels forever. Trust me, I will create a better existence for all of us. Whereas Abba only wants to be loved - I will give the angels complete freedom to enjoy their own free will as they see fit...."

He stopped when he noticed they were all looking at him as if he were an absolute lunatic. *But they were the crazy ones.* And then, knowing it was about to become quite messy, he decided to do his old friend Gabriel one last favor, so that there would be no confusion later on. He knew he was about to shock all with what was to come next.

And with that decision, there would never again be the chance of going back for all eternity.

His gut filled with the glory of his own rebellion. The idea of total freedom became an exponentially-charged flight of soul. *And it would all begin this very moment in time with one simple act ....*

With a flick of his wrist, his spear slung from across his shoulder and struck Gabriel's neck. In the back of his mind, Lucifer wondered if Gabriel knew this was his last act of friendship for his one true friend. As Gabriel stumbled away, Abba rose to His feet.

Lucifer tried to see His face once and for all, but the illumination was too great, as it always had been. Instead, he readied his spear and then rocketed it into the air, *charging directly at the man he once called father.*

And that is when Yeshua stood from His throne and waved his right hand, immediately issuing forth a bolt of lightning directed at Lucifer's feet. Its charge hit the ground of Third Heaven right in front of Lucifer, stopping him dead in his tracks. The spear meant for Abba fell harmlessly to the ground.

For the first time anyone could ever remember, Yeshua's face became a scowl. His voice was angry and without pause. *"How art thou fallen from heaven, O Lucifer, son of the morning!"* Yeshua rose high into the air just before Lucifer, whose knees soon buckled. He had never counted on Yeshua's might. *"How art thou cut down to the ground, which didst weaken the nations! For thou hast said in thine heart, I will ascend into heaven – Our very throne. I will exalt my throne above the stars of God: I will sit also upon the mount of the congregation, in the sides of the north: I will ascend above the heights of the clouds; I will be like the most High ...."*

Yeshua shuddered with vehemence as He raised his right hand once again. *"Yet thou shalt be brought down to hell, to the sides of the pit."*

However, before Yeshua could act, Lucifer's fear had caused him to stumble backwards, whereupon he tripped over something behind his feet and went tumbling right out of the throne room; in fact, right out of Third Heaven itself....

***

Asher hobbled down, the call of conflict ringing in his ears. By some measure, by some intervention from Abba, he had escaped from Lucifer's plan, and now he hobbled towards the only safe place he knew. The home of Midian, one of the more zealous angels around. If he was not in battle, then he was resting in his favorite abode within the vast Garden of Praise.

He just needed a place to rest and tend to his wounds. It was strange though, the more he walked, or trudged along, holding his injured side, it was as if there was a light behind his eyes, and he felt like there was an echo ringing behind his ears.

He pushed the thought out of his mind, and finally found Midian's modest living quarters, which were made of fine marble.

Asher made a mental note to apologize for breaking in, but at the moment, he needed healing, and more importantly, sustenance. In all of the life given to him by Abba, never before had Asher felt such discomfort - he could not remember having ever felt pain whatsoever. If this was what it would be like for the humans to come, then Asher pitied them already. *They will have a tough road to bear and will need every bit of prayer and help from Abba, Yeshua, and Eliezer they can muster, even if most of that help might eventually come through us, as directed by Abba.*

"Then again," he muttered to himself, "perhaps I should pity myself." *We have entered dark times, all of us....*

He had been foolish and arrogant, and now he was paying the price. As Asher managed to hobble through Midian's home, he found a healing drought located beneath an armorer's bench. Immediately, he poured it onto his wounds.

Sitting still and waiting for the elixir to do its magic, he considered, once again, how he had escaped. For the most part, it was all still a blur, a confusing mess. He remembered throwing a punch, fighting his way out, but other than that… it seemed too easy, as if they had wanted him to depart.

Not quite being able to put a finger on it, he shook his head, trying to clear his thoughts and vision.

Something still confused him greatly … but he had other things to focus on at the moment, and the main one being, *not dying.*

The sword which then suddenly became leveled at his throat made him rethink that notion, and now added great doubt that he would succeed.

"Ally, or enemy?" A familiar voice asked.

"Ally to Abba, enemy to rebels," Asher replied, without flinching.

With that, the sword was lowered, and Midian stepped into view.

"Asher," he said, then after a moment's pause, embraced his brother. "It's good to see you. We thought they were going to kill you once we understood that you had been captured and were being held captive!"

"And I thought the same for many nights," Asher replied. "I was held by Zared's men, under Lucifer's direct orders, but to be truthful, Zared was ready to kill me then and there. *It had been Lucifer who had spared me, for whatever the reason.* I only recently managed to escape, but something still does not seem right."

Midian frowned momentarily. "How was it then, that you had managed to secure your own escape?"

"I was just contemplating that very occurrence the moment I felt your sword upon the nape of my neck. Truth is, *I...do not know,*" No matter how hard he racked his brain, no answer would come to Asher. With a shake of his head, Asher looked to Midian, "I..."

Midian shook his head. "It does not matter, come with me." And he motioned for Asher to follow.

In a hazy and somewhat numbing fog, Asher followed Midian out of his home, and back out into the once peaceful Second, now he supposed, Third Heaven. *Will there ever be peace again - our home, now disturbed and remiss of the sole purpose it had previously for all eternity until now - devotion and love for Abba, and Abba's care and love for us.* As they walked, a sudden throbbing ran through Asher's skull, forcing him to have to stare upward.

Streaking through the sky like a giant fireball, tearing down from Third Heaven like an exploding morning star, was a comet unlike anything Asher had seen before. He turned briefly to Midian, who was staring up at it as well, his mouth gaping open in shock.

Asher did not know why, but at that moment, he felt a strange sensation in his chest, one not unlike pain, regret, or even remorse. Staring at the descending ball of fire, he identified the pain more accurately, and he realized that it was sorrow. But moreso, to refine its specific origins even further, it was ... *finality* - like someone or something had crossed a threshold from which they could never return.

And for the life of him, the pain in his chest festered until he felt as if it might explode, and Asher could not help shaking the notion that for the first time in the history of the Heavens, something rather absurdly harrowing, gruesome, heinous, and macabre, and yet also uniquely original, had taken place ....

Finally succumbing to the atrocity he felt within his soul, Asher fell to the ground. Midian rushed over to him and picked him up. "W-what was that?" Asher asked through pained and thorny breaths.

"I don't know," Midian replied.

"Was that—that Lucifer?" Asher asked, disbelieving his own intuition and yet realizing the festering wound within his heart was telling him such, and this could only be caused by something close to its actuality.

"I don't know," Midian said curtly, but then realized Asher might very well be right, and that he himself was now feeling such a sharp pain in his chest, though not to the extent to which Asher had obviously felt it.

Asher tried getting to his feet but could only do so with Midian's help. As they began walking, Asher asked, "You feel it, too. It was Lucifer, wasn't it?"

"I don't know, I don't know, and *I don't know,*" Midian answered, each repetition more forceful and daunting as the one before it. It had scarcely been more than a few minutes since they had witnessed the morning star falling, and yet, each second that passed only came with more questions for each of them. It was no use discussing further, and so all of their questions went unanswered.

Asher and Midian trudged along, feeling a bit stronger with each step. However, Asher was growing more concerned with every new breath. Feeling his friend's angst, Midian was finally forthcoming and honest. "Just before I found you at my home, the word had gone out. Gabriel's legions had been sent throughout every corner of Second

Heaven to give us the news. We are to gather all angels whose loyalty has been usurped by Lucifer and Zared."

"What are we to do with them once we gather them?"

Midian considered the calmness inherent in Asher's tone. "My brother, do not for one moment believe they will come to us willingly, or will follow our directives to be contained."

Asher looked at him and realized what was to come: it was as if another lance was striking his heart and he was at the end of his ability to cope.

Soon enough, Midian stopped in front of a tree along the path they had been taking, held out his hand in front of Asher, then tapped on the trunk twice. Asher blinked - there was nothing in the tree, nor around it, below it, nor above it. For all that he knew, this tree in Heaven was just that, a tree.

So, when Midian went around the tree and didn't appear on the other side, Asher was quite befuddled. With confusion digging into his already pained side, Asher stumbled in the same direction as Midian went, and as he circled the tree, he suddenly became quite surprised at what was there before him.

He had to blink to make sure his eyes were not deceiving him. But they reported the same thing: *Midian and other angels stood and crouched, tending to those with wounds.* It was then that it clicked for Asher. Whatever magic was used to enshroud them made for an effective hideout to tend to the wounded.

"What is this?" he asked Midian.

"Our little hideout," Midian answered. "Come, there is much to discuss, and you still need to be seen by a healer. But then, we need to move, and quickly."

"Quickly?" Asher followed Midian down along a marble path, at one point, avoiding bumping into another angel who was rushing back towards the entrance tree. "I do not like the sound of that. What else is about to happen?"

"Isn't it obvious?" Midian stopped and turned to him, then gestured towards rows of newly created arms and armor. *"Further battle."*

***

Elsewhere, Zared smiled as he watched all of the fighting throughout Second Heaven. *Sometimes battle is cleansing. In time, we will have all that we had ever wanted.* The spell Lucifer had cast on that fool Asher had proven to be a great boon. So long as that spell remained, then they would always have a way to see just what those loyalist fools were planning. And now, they were preparing for something quite large and exciting to come. Watching it all through Asher's eyes, Zared chuckled to himself - *they didn't suspect a thing.*

It was a good thing they let Asher go, how else would they have known?

Joash returned from the fields just then and immediately came to Zared. "You are in charge, now!"

Zared turned and immediately knew the truth: Lucifer had fallen from Third Heaven and had ceased to stop when he had passed through Second Heaven, meaning ...."

"We have confirmation that Lucifer is down on this place called earth, something I regret to dignify by calling it First Heaven," Joash said.

Zared nodded. "I am very well prepared." He then motioned to his commanding generals to ready their troops at once. *There is yet one last battle which we will fight and then prevail.* Once again, he chuckled.

***

"Napthali," Ammon said, "there is something I wish to discuss with you."

"Speak then," Napthali replied, "and I will thus answer thee, so long as I can."

They flew to the site of the Pearly Gate, where other traitors had recently been spotted. Abba had already repaired the gate, and it looked better than before, more ceremonious and decorative, with golden leaves attached to the pearl bars, and newly etched marble inlays implanted upon the stone pillars.

The falling star which had descended through the heavens and had last been seen much earlier, had now disappeared from the sky. Every angel in existence was attempting to discern its origins, and while they were all very concerned and more than a little curious, they had other, more pressing matters to attend to.

"What do you think Gabriel and Michael will do?" Ammon asked. "These rebels, these traitors, have spilled the blood of our own, and have gone against Abba's plan. Yet, our two commanding leaders have taken no action."

"They...they have taken the actions they deem necessary," Napthali replied. "I do not know what Michael wishes to do, but Gabriel will join us, of that, I am certain."

"Hm, then what of the Cherubs? I have yet to see them join us in battle."

"Not everyone is a fighter, brother," Napthali returned. "Some serve other roles."

"You may be correct; however, it seems likely that their spirits are crushed now, together with our own, with this turn of events. Has the power of praise itself been diminished?" Ammon wondered.

"Never, my brother. Never.... Some may wish it was so because they do not have the same goals as Abba does - either for themselves or for the heavens. That is the very trick in one complete thought: they desire their own free will above Abba's itself, and thus, have given into the dual temptations of self-inclination along with the belief in their own power. Abba had given us free will so that we might see that turning it back over to Him was our true goal."

They were silent for a moment or two while Ammon considered all that Napthali had said. Each glanced around themselves to see if any traitors were in sight, but they could see none within their field of vision.

"Then, tell me," Ammon finally said, "what do you think of the Seraphim? He has done nothing but worship since he was created. I do not consider that he will take to battle either. Is his role just as important as ours?"

Napthali looked at Ammon with a slight grin. "That was my very next statement. You took the words right out of my mouth!" Napthali nodded slightly. "I would venture to say that in Abba's view, his role, along with that of all of the cherubims, is much more important than our own. In fact, I would love to join them in their prayers, in their devotion and songs of praise, but at this time, we need warriors and soldiers, not worshippers alone. What good are devotions when heaven itself is falling apart? Those who remain locked with their hands clasped cannot defend themselves."

"Then … *why won't He defend them?*" Ammon asked, hesitantly, and not wanting to seem disgruntled.

"I do not know, I suppose." Napthali said, disappointed in himself that he could provide no clear answer. "Nobody can know the mind of Abba, Yeshua, and Eliezer. Nobody can guess at their grand plan."

"Here is what I think," Ammon said. "Abba cannot complete His plan without the cherubim and the Seraphim. Their worship sustains Him, and is required to make His new world as He sees fit. Together, their songs of worship and devotion, along with all of their praise, carry the Throne itself. I truly believe that they alone shall be set to guard the Garden."

Just then, several more loyalist angels dropped in from on high, Asher being one of them. He had overheard the last part of the conversation. "Garden?" Asher's shaky and weary voice called. *"What Garden?"*

"Hello, Asher, nice to see you back within the ranks of the faithful. I meant the Garden of Eden," Ammon answered. "It is to be a paradise in the making, according to several Cherubs with whom I had the pleasure of speaking. I had heard them planning their great works to come. These humans will learn to love and praise Abba through their examples."

"That sounds, to me, like a wonderful gift," Asher called. "When will it be ready?"

"I do not know," Ammon replied, his brow furrowed. "I presume when the first humans will walk upon the Earth. Beyond that, I cannot say."

Asher fell silent, as did the rest of their group. Napthali's expression remained stern and concerned, and it reminded them all of their mission. One last moment of quiet, before they once again would meet their fallen brothers upon the field of battle.

The silence was heavy, far more than what Ammon wanted to bear. No longer could they call their home in heaven untainted, and forevermore, it would be stained with the blood of those they had once called *brother*. Lucifer and Zared, all the others, weakened solely because of their jealousy infecting them and wounding their pride.

But, then again, Ammon was willing to admit that they were not entirely at fault in their defection. Abba, despite His wisdom, had in fact done nothing to ease the pain of those who were affected by their own shortcomings. Those who had professed loyalty, only to have it turned on its head despite doing everything that was asked of them. Or had they been? Maybe there was more, much more, to it than Ammon would ever know. If known how deep the dissension had become, perhaps there would have been a way to see that these events progressed more peacefully. *Then I could have understood the rebels' defection, perhaps even seen them off and assisted them in finding a new home.*

But the moment they stopped being my brothers was the moment they spilled the blood of our very kin. No argument, no cause, no reason was enough to justify the act of violence against family. If there was a dispute, then harsh words would be exchanged: anger was understandable. But violence? And leaving Abba for all time, as well? Despite how foreign that idea seemed, it was now a reality.

Ammon knew in his heart that he could never forgive the rebels for their crimes. If they had wanted to leave, they should have just left. He would gladly have seen them out, with no ill wishes upon them. But now? *No. There could be no mercy for those who had none themselves.*

Ammon clasped his weapon tighter within his grip as a shadow fell over him. He glanced up to see Gabriel, greatsword in hand, flying down to meet them. "Archangel Gabriel," Ammon said, almost breathlessly. "You wish to join us?"

Gabriel said nothing for a moment, his gaze cast in the direction where the falling star had last been seen. "I...wish to convey the message of most importance to Abba's Kingdom." He looked at each of the soldiers gathered together within the group. "*The time is at hand.* We must now save what remains of our family, round-up the traitors and throw them out," he said. "Ready yourselves, there is now no turning back."

Naphtali was the first who nodded, "To battle, then."

"Aye," Gabriel muttered. *"To battle."*

***

They went straight to the camp of the rebel angels which were in the fields adjacent to the Jesuviah Gardens. So many angels were below them, all of them standing within ranks and formations.

"There are thousands of them," Napthali said.

"Gird your loins, brothers," Gabriel responded. He looked back and counted maybe two-hundred loyalists with him. Michael had many more, wherever he was at this time. And others would soon be called to join them.

Gabriel was a soldier, and as such, he had the training and in practice, he was no stranger to battle. He was familiar with the web and flow of combat; when to give, when to take, and how to notice when events weren't shaping up the way they were supposed to. *None of this had been necessary until now.*

Lucifer's men saw their approach and responded by acquiring tactical formation.

Gabriel motioned and half of his army flanked to the left, and the other half, to their right. With his right hand he commanded descent, and immediately, the angels responded.

When they began engagement, it seemed surreal. Immediately, weapons which had been used for practice up until now, suddenly became charged with life-or-death importance. Ammon took on the first commanding officer he could find. With his sword drawn high in one hand and his shield protecting him and being held firmly in the other, he commanded, "Surrender now to the ranks of Gabriel or Michael, pledge your allegiance to us, or if not, you have one opportunity to come with me peacefully and avoid having to be forced!"

With that, the commanding officer, the rebel named Jael, made a turn to back away. But just as soon as he had, he quickly drew his spear from his side, dashed down in a quick semicircle back around, and flew up at Ammon, bringing the spearhead directly at his heart. Ammon was able to slash his sword down just in time to deflect it, however, he took a glancing blow to his side as the tip came just up between his plates of armor. He came back with his sword to deliver an uppercut to Jael, but the rebel had backed away and deflected it with his shield. They continued exchanging barbs back and forth ....

Meanwhile, Midian was combatting two rebels simultaneously. With arrows falling all around him, he protected himself with his armor and covered his head with his shield; however, this left him exposed to the danger from his enemies' swords. Flailing his own sword in mighty swings back and forth from his left to his right, the noise from the clanking weapons was incessant. Midian took a charging step forward at each fallen angel, and then would withdraw back to keep balance. He had lost regard for the foe before him: no longer brothers, they were enemies intent on his destruction, and so he willed himself to forego his conscience in order to deliver the force necessary for his survival.

As for Gabriel, he, Naphtali, Kenite, and Heber had approached a crowd of perhaps ten rebels, asking them to lay down their weapons and to come with them to be presented to Michael for relocation. The rebels laughed and then drew their weapons, at which point, they charged at Gabriel and his brothers. That was the start of when the attack became generalized all at once, as every rebel angel sought a loyalist faction and vice versa. Battles broke out across the fields as far as any angel could see. The four loyalist brothers had to form a circle of defense as mobs of rebels closed in on them. With their shields and weapons before them, they had been attempting to launch a counter-offensive against any rebel who came too close.

Lucifer's rebels had proven themselves to be a hardy bunch. What they lacked in discipline, they made up for in raw ferocity and individual cunning. This made it a challenge to find appropriate tactics - when one rebel might have been a conventional fighter, another would be a devious trickster who was using his allies as shields to accomplish his goals. However, this meant that what the rebels had in power, they lacked as far as unity. And without a cohesive fighting force, even while under the pressure within the tightening circle surrounded by throngs of rebels, Gabriel figured that they would be overwhelmed, sooner or later. *But if that was the case, why do I have such a chill running down my back?*

Just outside of Yeshuva Garden proper, Zared smiled. Watching it all taking place through Asher's eyes, he was happy that Asher had taken the wise choice to observe from afar, and not get involved directly with any of the battles beyond a few long-range attacks here and there. Even though Asher's attacks with his bow and arrows, made of gold and silver with fire and ice arrowheads, did hit several rebels when Zared wasn't able to warn them in time about Asher's approach, *that was a small price to pay for having such a clear view of the battlefield.*

Napthali called out a command, and soon the four loyalists entrapped within the throngs of rebels all took to a straight arrow formation. With Gabriel leading, they began pushing through the rebels' lunatic and absurdly contradictory mob. As they strode further along, Gabriel swung his large greatsword with a ruthless efficiency that was brought on by desperation and betrayal. Beheading three rebel angels, he had become frantic. Watching heads roll was nothing to him, and presently he looked all about, but Michael was nowhere to be seen. He turned back to glance over his shoulders at his comrades, and just then, he felt Abba suddenly calling each of them home.

As the multitude of battles raged on, Gabriel took to the air, followed soon thereafter by his three brothers. Gabriel kicked at the heads of the fallen angels as he rose above the three who had given him quite a struggle. These rebels could fly, but they had been ordered to stand their ground and to not retreat from their positions. "We have all been called away to see Abba," Gabriel declared, God's messenger, who would receive messages from the Elohim routinely directly into his mind. He looked down once at the thousands of battles taking place just below them. *Even without him, the loyalist angels were all fighting with a vigor that was an even match for the rebel's fury.*

Unfortunately, one of the last things he saw before they would be too distantly far to see anything below them, was an especially cruel manifestation of rebel conscience. As one of their dear brothers was battling sword-to-sword and rather handily with one of the rebels, another unseen rebel came waltzing towards them with his spear raised high above him. The loyalist could not see him sneaking up from behind, and as he unknowingly raised his sword to strike at the heart of the rebel in front of himself, this new, Pro-Lucifer angel dug the icy top of his spear beneath the loyalist's back plate right through the opening just at the top of his neck. This sent the angel flying to the ground, wriggling in misery and pain. A moment later, Gabriel saw that the angel had bled out and had stopped flailing altogether.

But vigor could be broken, and a push could be halted if there was something that could provide enough leverage. This is what now concerned Zared the most, especially since three of his generals, Abib, Gadder, and Sabib, had told him that if Gabriel was the sword, *then Michael was the one who guided it.*

Known throughout Second Heaven as the kind, benevolent angel, Michael kept people together, and so without him, Zared concluded, the loyalists would fall apart. After all, no creature could exist without their heart and soul.

So, where was…? Zared locked in again on Asher's vision as Asher's gaze drifted to the east, where a single angel stood under a tree, far from the battle. *Michael.* Zared smiled and motioned for several angels to follow him. It was time to take another captive, and who better a captive than Archangel Michael?

With speed and purpose, carried also by a mixture of desperation and hope, Zared and these other rebel angels took to the air as a plan formed in Zared's mind.

***

Gabriel kneeled, and cursed himself under his breath. Abba had called him back, perhaps He had seen that the round-up of Lucifer's rebels was not proceeding as planned. *As if it were that simple, if only because the rebels had proven themselves to be stubborn, if nothing else.*

"My son," Abba said, "tell me, how does the battle go?"

"The rebels have organized well, and as such, have both a tactical and a personal advantage, since battle is new to those loyal to you, Father," Gabriel said. "I imagine that it will take several more days to draw them out completely, hopefully without either side suffering many casualties."

"I see," Abba said.

Gabriel kept his gaze focused on the ground. "I fear that this battle will be one of many."

He felt Abba nodding affirmation.

Another pair of angels approached in haste. One of them called, "We have lost sight of Archangel Michael!"

Gabriel rose to his feet. "What of his guards?"

"We don't know!" the angel said. "We don't know! Sir, what do we do?"

Gabriel gritted his teeth. "Take a squad and head to Michael's last known location, do not let him come to harm under any circumstance."

"Sir!" The angels rose to their feet, and Gabriel frowned. He felt as if he was losing patience. First Lucifer had turned, and now

Michael was in danger of being lost. If the worst happens to Michael then, at this rate, he would be the last archangel standing.

"Hm, what sadness is this?" Abba's words shook Gabriel out of his worries. "I made you to be a leader, and now it seems you are a commander."

Gabriel blinked. "I apologize, sire, I am just questioning myself. *Did I make a mistake?*"

Abba shook his head. "No, no ... these are forces which are completely independent of you and your actions."

Abba turned his head to the side, and a thought occurred to Gabriel. Here in front of him, stood the most powerful being of all creation in Three Persons, who managed to cast out Lucifer, his brother, with barely a flick of his wrist. *Why could He not help them directly? Sap the rebels of their will to fight? Cast them down out of the heavens altogether?*

These were the traitorous, angered thoughts of a child, Gabriel knew this, but even so, he still had them. "My father," he said, "I have a question."

"You wish to ask why I do not intervene directly?" Abba asked and smiled slightly as Gabriel's face flickered with surprise. "Do not be alarmed, yes I feel your thoughts, as you know, but in this instance, yours were written all over your expression."

"I...yes," Gabriel nodded.

Abba sighed. "I wish to, I wish to end this pointless conflict, and by some measure, I could. But what would that make me? Lucifer feared me as a tyrant, and I share the same fears. If I were to exercise My will as a combatant, indeed, I could end this conflict in a matter of seconds. But what of the aftermath? What would they think? The Angels who remain with me would know that I could do the same to them at a moment's notice, and the rebels who remain would still seek vengeance against me for interfering with their free will. As much as I wish for it, I cannot end this by myself."

Gabriel nodded. "I understand Father." He bowed. "I fear I must now return to battle, before too much else is lost."

"Yes, My son. Go -," Abba replied.

With that, Gabriel stood and left the room. He had to get back to the battle, to turn the tide, or at the very least, help in any way he could. As soon as he turned the corner and came through the Pearly Gates of Third Heaven, his vision became filled with the black shaft of a pole.

Is that a spear? Gabriel thought a half instant before a shaft collided with his eyes. Reeling and turning, his vision now blurry, Gabriel fumbled for his greatsword just as he heard shouted words from his assailants. "Now, while he's disorientated!"

His eyes spiked with pain, but his arms still worked, and his feet were happy to move. Kicking off the stone underneath, Gabriel jumped back, and narrowly avoided the whistle of a blade rushing past his neck, the only unarmored part of his body. Spinning and pivoting, Gabriel raised his right arm high, his greatsword pitched and pending discharge.

"Traitors!" he snapped, and as his hand clasped the metal handle of his sword, a rebel's longsword had been in momentum and aimed right at a small spot where no plate armor lay between his forearm and hand. The blade found its mark, but the linking chain underneath protected Gabriel's flesh. *It stung him all the same.* Gabriel snapped his right arm down and caught the rebel who had struck him across the neck with a glancing blow. Using muscles long since honed by ages past, Gabriel slammed the traitor down onto the pavement. Cracks spread throughout the once pristine floor, marble floor. *A part of Gabriel hated that he couldn't tell which action he regretted more, shattering the stone or the person who was once his brother.*

"Kill him!" Another yelled.

Gabriel spun, turned, and was in position to overcome his enemies. As his hand once more raised his sword, he had a thought which permeated him completely. *They do not understand my power. I will try to defend myself with my hands alone, except when necessary, that is the least I can do for the angels who were once my kin.*

***

Michael wasn't the same kind of fighter that many of the other angels were, indeed, his weapons were most often his words, not his fists. But even so, he knew better than anyone that sometimes, words could only carry a person so far, and as such, he had learned to use the weapon given to him by Abba with utmost care. A mighty longsword of gold and silver, adorned in ice along its shiny and sharp blade, but also covered with fire when the weapon struck. *A magnificent weapon by all accounts.*

Wrestling with his conscience, figuring how to kill a fellow angel, a former brother, concerned him to no end. Yes, he knew his duty and knew he would persevere, and the time had come to do battle. Standing from his respite, he was focussing on a squad of forty rebels gaining ground with ten loyalist brothers in the meadow to the east of *Eliezer Hill. Yes, a fitting name for the place of my first victory.*

Suddenly he heard a familiar voice from behind him. *"Archangel Michael!"* Zared yelled. "How good to see you. Enjoying the show?"

"No," Michael said, turning to face his enemy. "I do not enjoy the sight of one brother harming another."

"Is that so?" Zared tilted his head. "I must admit, I could get rather used to it."

Michael eyed the twenty angels as they surrounded him. He tried stalling for time so that he could plan his best course of action. *"What do you want?"* Michael asked, even though he already knew the answer.

Zared put on a false smile. "Why, your time, of course."

"Of course," Michael said, and raised his blade. Turning slowly in a full circle to confront his potential assailants with his sword at the ready, he realized this was about to get very bloody.

"We don't have to do this," Zared said, as his lackeys closed in on Michael.

"No, your kind wants nothing more than to harm and hurt," Michael returned.

Zared shrugged. "Fair enough." He then smiled and motioned to his allies. "Take him."

Michael got in three quick swings of his sword, but each only managed to be deflected by the shields and armor of the rebels he had hit. By that time, five more came from behind and wrestled him to the ground, where they bound his feet and hands tightly with bow strings.

***

It was a strange thing; to fall. For as long as Lucifer had been alive, he had known the sensation, of course. Of letting himself drift across the sky without bothering to carry himself on the currents. Yet, he had never known himself to truly 'fall' in the sense that he had no control over his descent whatsoever.

He had tripped, fallen over the altar of heaven, cast out by his father, and was sent like a falling star through the air. Fire coated him, as he called upon whatever strength he had to defend himself as he was hurtled downwards. It took all of his might not to be burnt to a crisp from Abba's last act, but even so, through the fire and the air, Lucifer was still able to see, albeit dimly.

There, his forces, his rebels, fought the loyalist forces of Abba, and it was hard to tell who was winning. He caught sight of Gabriel, hefting his greatsword and cutting through another one of his men.

Asher was there as well, no surprise, given that he caught flickers of what the loyalists were doing through his eyes. That spell had proven to Lucifer that in order to win this war, this uprising, then strength alone wasn't enough, power would only see them be crushed by a God on high.

No, cunning, wit, and skill, those were the things we needed.

He had made the mistake of thinking that power would protect him in the throne room and look what happened. He had fallen, struck down by Abba's hand, all because he had made the nonsensical, prideful choice to engage Abba one-on-one. As he considered his fall, he realized he had remained within some forcefield which had taken him to his destination, plunging him downwards through a strong portal - a stargate which, Lucifer reasoned, connected everything in Abba's universe, including earth.

There must be many more of these such stargates.

As Lucifer Morningstar was falling, he swore to himself to no longer play the part of a fool. As the clouds had passed by him, as Heaven fell away, Lucifer's eyes had closed as minutes, maybe hours, had passed. He wasn't sure anymore. However, while falling through the stargate, the air had become quite different. It was no longer pleasantly cool, but instead achingly hot, and then at one point, all of his weapons and his armor suddenly caught fire, burnt up and then had dissipated into the atmosphere.

What a fool I had been, but a fool I will no longer continue to be ...

Time ceased to mean anything to him. He fell for only Abba knew how long, and then, suddenly, he had hit the ground, and for the first time in Lucifer's long life, he knew what it was like to taste sand.

More importantly, he knew how to beat Abba at His own game ....

Chapter Eight

It was safe to say that Michael was never a warrior, never a fighter. Oh, sure, he could fight, if need be, but his best weapons had always been his words. A fact he was keenly aware of as Zared's blade cut across his cheek, and as he arched backwards, still bound, to avoid a blow from yet another rebel.

"Traitor!" Michael snapped.

"Blind fool!" Zared returned. Zared looked at the scowl on Michael's face - his raw hatred and determination. "You want to dance, Michael? Is that what you would like? I was going to simply hold you captive to see what meager heroes might come to try and rescue you, that was my original intention. However, say the word and I will free you and we can fight it out, brother. *Would you like that?"*

"I would like anything which disrupts your plans, you scum."

"How dare you insult me when you are right now at my mercy. Don't you believe I could end your miserable, devotional life, this very second?"

"If you do, Abba will still find a way to send you to a place brimming with the fire of hatred which you have sown. A place for all of your kind – where you can be chained for all eternity watching as the remainder of us who are loyal and devoted live in Heaven peacefully and sharing the bond of unity and brotherhood as had been intended by Abba all along."

"Oh, how I grow so weary of hearing you repeat your incessant chants of praise to Abba. Abba who is going to replace you and Abba who has made you imperfect from the day you came into existence." Zared turned to his army of men. "Now I leave you no choice, *brother*. Let's see once and for all how Abba will save you in battle. Let's see if I can end your misery right here and right now." With a nod, five of Zared's men loosened the bowstrings which had kept Michael bound.

Zared drew his sword and charged along with many of his fellow rebels. Michael reached to the ground and raised his longsword to defend himself as a blow raked across his blade, sending shudders up his arm. He tried for a stab at one of the fallen angels, and found his half-ready blow was deflected by the rebel using his shield, and his blade was battered aside. Michael had to use all of his strength just to hold onto his sword.

With each passing second, he had to give more and more ground just to keep them all in his sights and to assure not a single one of them could flank him. While he was certain that he could defeat any one of them in single combat, including Zared, the simple fact of the matter was that the rebels were smart enough to keep surrounding him, attempting to take advantage of his blind spots.

And due to this, Michael returned to the air. His intention was to come around and then drop right in front of Zared, taking him on one-to-one. However, Zared and his rebels followed in the air directly after him. Michael would not run from his task and so he changed course and charged right at them.

With all his might, he slashed his sword at one rebel after another. Mostly hitting their armor, he caused them to pause in their pursuit of him momentarily, but not much more than that. The sounds of clanking swords filled the air. And still, the rebels encircled Michael, closing in on him quickly. One after another, Michael deflected their attempts to kill him. Zared was in the second row of angels, watching with glory as Michael came ever closer to exhaustion, wherein he would no longer be able to defend himself.

Michael then saw an angel he vaguely knew as Joash, who had sensed his weakness, had begun to reel back to launch his spear with all his might. The armor and weapons made by Abba were unsurpassed in all of creation, but that also meant that they were equal to each other. While a sword at the wrong angle might not cut through the armor, the spear's pointed blade could, if thrown at just the right spot, and at just the right amount of strength.

Michael realized he would not be able to deflect both the blades of swords coming at his neck, along with Joash's spear being thrust at him, all at the same time. Joash had recoiled and now let go with a frightful thrust of his spear. A second later, Michael realized that the spear would hit its mark, which was right in his flank. As blood spilled out of his side, he doubled over and called out, "Abba!" He had never before known pain. His flight was cut short, and he began a downward spiral, descending so quickly that he did not have time to prepare as he hit the ground. The brutal impact caused his weapon to dislodge from his hands and it went flying away from him.

Skidding along the ground, he finally came to a stop at the crest of a tree.

He let out a pained gasp, and gingerly reached to where he had been struck. The spear had fallen out as he had crashed, leaving the wound to open more as the friction of the ground ripped away at it. Given enough time, he could have healed it in a moment.

Could have, if not for Zared and his rebels soon landing on the ground a few feet away from him.

"Oh, how the mighty have fallen," Zared said. "Archangel Michael, Abba's favored diplomat. Tell me something wordsmith, where is your father now?"

Michael glared at Zared and clasped his hands together.

Zared nodded at his soldiers, who then proceeded to deliver one might blow after another onto Michael's torso, face, and back. His armor loosening under the pressure, Michael took repeated stings of lances, spears, and swords.

Zared laughed out loud. "Go on, Michael, mighty warrior for God. Go on now and show us your might. You are weakened and are about to fall for all eternity. Everyone everywhere will know you as the beaten and decimated warrior of Abba!"

As he lay on the ground, Zared came over and began kicking him mercilessly on the head. Michael rolled over, blood spilled across the ground and covered his armor.

"Haha! *Go on Michael, make your move!*" Zared continued.

Still with his hands clasped, Michael began to utter a prayer. "Father, Abba... I come to you now with all sincerity of purpose and heart. I know you can do everything, and no thought can be withholden from thee. You know my needs and yet, I know you desire me to ask it of you directly and with full confidence." Still taking a thorough beating, and almost near death, he continued, "I need your strength, Lord, I need you to impart within me that same strength right at this moment. May I have what it will take to defeat these - our enemies? *Abba, Father, I ask you now at this moment to grant me the gifts of warfare....*"

***

Elsewhere, in a silent room, Michael's words reached a patient and concerned ear, and that listener decided enough was enough. He would not interfere directly, but He could lend strength to those who needed it. Abba watched from afar and had been ready, hoping Michael would have asked such of Him.

Beside Abba, Yeshua turned a loving glance at His Father. "It has happened. Now the time has come."

Eliezer was between Father and Son, and He infused a powerful glance onto Michael.

Now, Abba raised His right hand and imparted Michael with all of the strength necessary, the skills, the knowledge and wisdom, and the mastery of battle to rid this heaven of evil once and for all.

***

Michael finished his prayer, and waited. Zared paused, looked to the left, then the right, and smiled. "Where is your god indeed? Where is that impotent fool you call a master?"

Michael closed his eyes and waited for whatever was to come.

"Nowhere, save that ivory tower," Zared said, and lifted his sword. "Now come, brother, show me what's on the other side of your so-called wisdom. Nothing! *You have nothing and into nothing you shall now perish!*" With all the speed and power granted by spite and scorn, Zared brought the sword down.

And at that very moment, Michael felt God's light upon him, and in that instant, he knew he had what was necessary. He knew what he had to do.... And Michael's hand snapped up to catch Zared's sword by the blade.

Zared stood in shock, as Michael's hand now firmly grasped around the blade of Zared's sword. Yet, the blade did not cut Michael's skin, not a drop of blood was drawn from his palm, as a golden aura now surrounded Michael. His wounds immediately healed, his armor restored, his shield in his left hand, and his mighty sword now held firmly within his right hand; he stood and arched up and above Zared.

"What?" Zared shrieked.

"Honestly," Michael shrugged. "I cannot believe you truly doubted Abba's power and His love for those who remain loyal. Did you truly believe He would let you win?" Michael's face hardened, and he was fully adorned in the heavenly light which shone all around him.

Even so, with a powerful tug of his arm, Zared's sword flew from his hand towards Michael's face. Michael easily deflected it with his shield, and then, with a much more powerful punch straight to Zared's jaw, Michael allowed himself a rare grin as Zared went flying backwards.

The assembled group of rebels gawked, their jaws hanging open in surprise and fear as Zared lay crumpled on the ground after hitting a rock at full speed.

***

Gabriel had rejoined the battle, and to the best of his knowledge, it hadn't been going all too well. The stalemate had ended in the rebel's favor, and now, the loyalist's battleline was being pushed back. Loyalists were doing their best to combat the rebels' assaults, and yet, nothing seemed to have been accomplished thus far besides blood and death.

At least, until an angel-shaped comet slammed into the ground just in front of the gate, drawing all of the assembled angel's attention as dust and debris plumed up upwards.

"What?" Gabriel said in surprise, his voice a whisper.

From out of the settling dust, a voice called, *"Brothers! Hear me!"*

Gabriel looked on high. There, flying in the clouds, encapsulated with Abba's might, was Archangel Michael.

He called now to his loyalist brethren. "No more shall we suffer their treachery, no more shall we suffer their wanton bloodshed! Follow me, my brothers, and we shall send them away from this heaven!" With that, Michael soared into the rebel's battleline, and scattered them all with naught but his sword of ice. They did not stand a chance, as Michael's force indemnified the energy around them, setting fire to their hatred and filling them with the fear of eternal damnation by Abba Himself.

For certainly with this show of power alone, to be cut-off from Abba's love for all eternity would be setting themselves against a power much greater than their own free will.

His words heeded, resounding within the collective mind of all of the loyalists, they rallied, and followed Michael into the fray once more. Within this umbrella of Michael's grace, they each had a newfound power and zeal. And so, with fury and now force, the loyalists collided anew against the rebels.

Gabriel swung his sword directly through the shield of a rebel, and found his own strength redoubled. No longer were his limbs and his mind set upon by doubt, and no longer weighted by despair: his muscles now burned with a vigor that had long before felt forgotten to him. With a swing of his greatsword, he cut down another rebel, and risked a half smile himself. "Michael!" he yelled, unsure if his brother could hear him, but willing to try. *"Where did this strength come from?"*

Gabriel had turned to search for his brother Michael, but then his ears perked at the shrill sound of a battle cry. Out of the corner of his eye, he saw a rebel, sword in hand, lunging directly at him, aiming to spill his blood all over the ground. He realized he had left himself wide open in that instant, and he would not be able to turn to defend himself from the sword's blade.

But then a sudden and satisfying kick from Michael sent the disgraced rebel flying away, and into the back of another. Michael landed next to Gabriel, and shouted for all to hear, *"Abba protects, just when you need Him the most."*

"Evidently!" Gabriel replied, and now stood beside Michael with renewed confidence. "Come then, let us now put an end to this battle."

"Gladly," Michael nodded, and they both rose in unison within the air once again. "I will end this battle with the strength given to me, to each of us, by our Lord."

With that, Michael took a deep breath, scouted the enemy's battlelines, then girded his loins and gritted his teeth. *For too long this battle has been raging, for too long my brothers have suffered under the corrupted, egotistical whining of others. Now, it is time for this battle to end.*

Michael spied the Gate and nodded. Inspired by Eliezer's spirit, an idea had come to him. *If the rebels wanted to leave Abba's embrace, then I will be all too happy to show them the door.*

With a plan in mind, it was time for Archangel Michael to show them why he was one of Abba's chosen few archangels.

He flew to the nearest rebel, a fool who was battling with shield and spear against a tiring loyalist. Michael caught the next thrust of the rebel's spear and took him by the throat. With a heave of his shoulders, strength powered by Abba's light, he twisted his waist, reeled his arm back, and with all of his might, hurled the rebel clear out of the battlefield, past the gate, and out of heaven altogether.

He, Gabriel, and every angel within sight spent the next few good seconds watching the rebel sailing through the air, his surprise and fear robbing him of his ability to fly. The rebel's face became filled with horror with the realization that he had no power against Michael's thrust. As his body passed through the gate, he became lost within a portal of light which sent him downwards until he was out of sight completely.

Michael turned his attention to the next rebel, where he repeated the process.

Soon, the rebels began to turn and run, but Gabriel flew with his squadron to meet and then interdict them. There was no escape for them now.

One by one, each of the Rebel's met Michael's grasp, and one by one, each of the rebels went sailing through the gate, and then into and down the portal. By Michael's newfound strength, each and every single rebel on the battlefield became little more than a sack of meat that was tossed out of heaven like the waste they had become. For hours, and then days, Michael did this.

He found each rebel that had tried hiding within the battlefield, or who were trying to blend within groups of their previous, still loyal, brothers. He tossed each and every one of them out of heaven, where they fell like their leader had.

That was a fitting punishment, Michael believed. If they wanted to become like Lucifer, then it was best for them to follow his example in learning the way out of heaven, and they too would fall like the morning star.

Once the last rebel had been found, Zared, Michael said a few words.

"You see now the power of God. Are you remorseful? Do you now wish you had never left His embrace?"

Zared turned to run, but Michael quickly overcame him and grasped his neck.

"Not to be so, rebel!" Michael looked him directly in the eye and Zared was repulsed. He began to vomit from his mouth. "Go and see your brother Lucifer. Give him a message from me: *He will never be victorious over any who remain loyal to Abba!"* Michael tightened his grip so that Zared could feel his own death - his eyes bulging out, his face purple, and his heart almost stopping completely within his chest.

Michael then lifted him and catapulted him out through the gate and into the portal.

They had now all been removed from heaven.

Michael released a last deep breath he had not even realized he had been holding tightly within his broad chest, and then he crossed his arms. He stood at the edge of heaven looking out, and before him was a cold and empty sky. Peering down, the last rebel finally became no more than a dot in his eyes, and then no matter how hard he looked, he was unable to find anyone, or anything, within the universe's vastness except for stars and planets. *Abba had created all of this when He had made earth - just so that earth, the new First Heaven, would not be alone. Magnificent!*

Gabriel suddenly approached, his once pristine armor was covered in dirt, blood, and grime. His shield was dented and worn, and his once bright silver and gold helmet now mostly coated in dark red.

"Brother," Gabriel's breaths came in heavy gulps. "Are...are you alright?"

After a moment's pause, Michael shook his head. "No."

"You've won," Gabriel continued. "The battle is over."

Michael shook his head once more, "Not yet."

Gabriel raised a brow, "Not yet?" he asked. "Brother, we have won. The rebels have been cast out, sent through Abba's portal to earth. What else is there to do?"

"Isn't it obvious, my brother?" Michael glanced at Gabriel. "To see this punishment through, to the end. They are free on earth now; the place Abba is to create mankind. More work is ahead for me, I fear. *I must construct a place wherein they never can have access to any man."*

***

Lucifer laid upon his back, his bones and muscles stiff, his skin pulsating with a new awareness of its exposure and vulnerability to the elements, and his pride left in more pieces than his once pristine armor. With a slow, thorny breath, he tried to stand. That's when he heard himself issue forth an utterance, which until now, he had been completely unfamiliar with since it had never before been heard by any of the angels. In his newfound discomfort, *Lucifer said, "Ugh."*

The blue sky loomed above him, not a cloud in sight. In a strange, painful way, it was peaceful. *What I have just heard from my own lips seemed more like a babel than a word. It is a new form of expression, and thus, this place will forever be known as Babel.*

With no Abba present to hold sway over him, no Michael to debate, and no more competing with Gabriel to prove who was the better fighter, Lucifer felt at ease for the first time in a long time. *Yes, no armies to fight … no more war to wage. Peaceful.*

"And yet, somehow," Lucifer narrowed his eyes, speaking words out loud for the first time since he had landed upon earth. *"I cannot stand it …figuratively speaking."*

He had 'sensed' the final outcomes which had occurred in heaven, the last vestiges of his divine power allowing him, through Asher's eyes, to see glimpses of the battles, no matter the distance. Even if it was shaky, at best, he had seen the last remnants of his forces fight, and lose, against Michael's sudden surge of strength. And in turn, he had seen his men be cast out, much like him. They were now falling down to earth, and in the back of his mind, Lucifer couldn't help but wonder whether or not this was part of Abba's plan all along.

He had set the stage for war, after all, and how quaint it was that just *now*, on the cusp of their victory, Abba finally saw fit to intervene.

Lucifer would have frowned if his facial muscles were working well enough, but at the moment, all his senses were numb, and he could manage only a slight drop of his lips.

"But this isn't the end," he said, or rather, muttered to himself. "I will come back, I will return." And then his voice raised an octave or two. "Do you hear me, Abba? I may lay upon the stony hardness of your abysmal creation *but believe me when I tell you that I will not stop until I make it my own.*"

As if responding to his proclamation, a small blip appeared above him, and Lucifer squinted as best he could. The blip grew larger and larger with each passing second, before he could finally discern that it resembled the outline of an angel. Then another blip appeared, and another, and another. Again, they grew to resemble outlines of his fallen brethren, and Lucifer blinked once. *"Oh, that's just quaint,"* he said.

The outlines become more detailed as the next moments passed, and Lucifer braced himself for the worst to come. He closed his eyes and held his breath. Then, the sounds of screaming filled his ears: some shouts of fright seemed familiar, while others were not, but all were like shrill daggers stabbing his ears, knives to Lucifer's soul.

First, they came one by one, then in pairs, and finally in small and large groups. Like smoldering explosions from a fire, his rebels began to fall to the sand all around him. Some landed face-first into the grainy sand of this new *Heaven,* others managed to land on their feet, and either way, most were then crushed with the weight of another hapless rebel crashing into them. Lucifer had nothing to do except count his breaths as the falling and screaming continued for hours on end, each second filled with the cries of his men.

Despite what Abba may have thought, he did not enjoy the sounds of his soldiers screaming and crying for help, and so, Lucifer made another promise, this time not to himself, but to his soldiers. He began shouting with all his voice, until his throat became raw and worn: *"Our humiliation will be paid back a thousandfold for Abba's support of Michael's transgressions against us!"*

Finally, the screaming stopped, and Lucifer gazed around. *How to rouse such a fallen battalion of soldiers?* It was useless for him to search for his commanding officers – surely, they were here amongst them somewhere. *But this must be a full third of all the angels Abba had ever created!* He closed his eyes for a moment and, in a sudden, reflexive action meant to diffuse his enormous amount of concern and uncertainty, he was about to pray to Abba for strength, support, and guidance!

"I must get over that," he said out loud.

Instead, he opened his eyes just as a flutter of wind caught his attention.

There, floating above him, above them all, was the criminal in question, Michael. He flew in the sky, miles above the landscape, which was littered for miles on end with rebels strewn every which way. As he floated above them, his expression was unreadable. Lucifer managed a frown, *just what was he planning?* Was Michael going to let out a speech? Some hogwash about Abba's light or love or some other trite nonsense?

The answer came when Michael spoke. His voice was clear, and yet as calm and as cold as the blade of fire and ice which ignited his sword. "You have harmed and murdered your own former brothers in the name of ideals that had not been well thought, which were never truly your own, and more than even that, you have betrayed the oaths you have sworn to uphold. For this, for your *sin,* I will see to it that you receive the punishment you have earned."

With nothing more to say, Michael flew to the edge of the field of rebels. With maddening fury, he plunged his hands into the earth again and again until he had begun to create a deep cavern. With a groan, his muscles straining as he pulled the earth aside, Michael continued his work at a fevered pace for quite some time. Repeatedly, he plunged his hands into the sea of sand, then flung them upwards, sending a wave of the coarse, rough substance behind him. Michael continued this, digging further and further down, until the lights in the heavens themselves began to lose their illumination.

Before long, his fingers touched bedrock, and Michael nodded. Plunging his fingers deeper still into the stone and rock, he grunted as he found purchase. Fractures spread throughout the bedrock, and with a surge of strength and pressure, it suddenly spread apart and gave way, making a gap wide enough for Michael to fit himself into. Then, placing his feet on one side, and pitting his back against the opposite wall, he pushed as hard as he could, both with his back and with his legs.

The ground shuddered, and then finally splintered and broke altogether, creating a large canyon underneath the sea of sand. Normally, this would have been impossible, even for an Archangel. But, with Abba's newest gifts bestowed upon him, Michael was able to make the impossible become an inevitability.

Suddenly, the fallen angels all felt the earth beneath them moving and shaking. The sand began shifting, all of it being drawn and sucked to the center of where Michael had been laboring. Lucifer was quite surprised when he realized what Michael had accomplished. Soon, he felt himself drawn within the vortex of shifting sand, and his back touched nothing but air. He let out a curse as his stomach lurched into his chest. *"How much more?"* he screamed. His answer came when his vision filled with nothing but sand, and he hit walls of rock on each side of him as he fell. His rebels all let out cries of anguish as they too fell into this new abyss.

"Michael!" Lucifer screamed. *"Is this your doing, or Abba's?!"*

His answer came when a red and orange portal opened behind him.

***

Michael had opened a new portal down to nearly the center of the earth. Above, the land had closed once again, covered with sand in every direction for as far as could be.

The very next thing Lucifer and all of his angels knew, they were being sucked down into and through this portal and arriving at their new dwelling. Lucifer's back suddenly hit molten stone and rock, and he tumbled along the ground for a few moments before coming to a hard and sudden stop against a fiery wall. Finally, Lucifer let out a wheeze, his head ringing as his hair fell over his shoulders. "Ugh," he groaned. *"Damn it all…"*

"Are you satisfied?"

Lucifer looked up and found himself in a small enclosure lined with rock and flames. It was barely large enough for him to walk around in. In fact, he could have spread his arms out, and almost touch each of the opposite walls. One wall was all bars made of iron, and on the other side of those bars was Michael, floating, as he often did.

"Damn you," Lucifer growled. *"Was digging that massive hole not good enough?"*

"That was to be the entrance, the portal, a gift from Abba, so that you may see the light that you so carelessly abandoned," Michael said.

Gabriel beckoned just then, and Michael felt his words. *"Abba has a message for you, stop, pray, and listen, Michael. I am coming to assist you and shall see you very soon."* Just as Michael had received renewed and permanent strength to defeat evil in all of its forms, Gabriel had become invested by Abba with the ability to deliver messages even when he was not directly in the presence of the one receiving it.

"You mean the light that held me back?" Lucifer growled, continuing his conversation with Michael.

Michael glared at Lucifer, but then did not respond. Instead, he listened to Gabriel's voice and went down to his knees, silently praying to Abba for His guidance and wisdom. A moment later, he received his answer. He stood and looked at Lucifer, wanting now to finish their final conversation. "You proclaim that Abba held you back, and that you had wished to be free," Michael tilted his head. "Yet, if that was the case, why did you choose to sign on with the betrayers, Lucifer? With those who had come to hate Abba due to their own insecurity and jealousy?"

"To be my own angel," Lucifer said. "To cease being beholden to the whims of some incompetent god."

"Then it seems only fair that you take responsibility for those actions," Michael said. "You say so much. In fact, your silver tongue is your greatest gift, *more so than any weapon or armor given to you.* But more than that, you lashed out because of some slight to your wounded pride. Tell me, even if your pride had not been wounded upon that day, would you have not tried some other plot, some other plan? Because your goal was not to distance yourself from Abba, no. You wanted more, much more than that. You wished to be *Him.*"

Just then, Gabriel became present beside Michael, having first traveled through the portal between Second and First Heaven, earth, and then through the newest portal created: from earth's surface down into Hell itself.

He immediately looked at Lucifer bound within the walls of fire and steel. His shame and his sadness became too much, and he could not find the words or necessity to speak to his former friend. Instead, he turned to Michael. "What, my brother, have you finished?" Gabriel asked. "I see you have found the power to create a lasting home for him and his companions."

"It is done," Michael said. "We are to return to Second Heaven, *for now.*"

Gabriel looked at Lucifer. Again, he wanted to express himself but found that he had no words to say, as words had proven to be nothing but useless to this one. Instead, he turned to Michael. "If that is Abba's will, then it shall be so …."

With that, Michael surprised them all when he turned back and then loosened the lock on the gate of Lucifer's dungeon. Gabriel stood in shock and was just about to protest, but Michael stopped him with a wave of his right hand.

They turned and took the portal back to earth's surface. It was a quick and easy transfer for the two loyal archangels, swift and comfortable. Once there, they waited, looking out across the vastness of sand in all directions. The earth was cold, dark, and devoid of all life and movement.

"It had all been so beautiful before … green and blue, and lush with growth, before Lucifer and his men were thrown down here onto its vast surface," Gabriel said.

"Yes, now it is so dark, and nothing lives… only rocks and boulders, with many mountains and valleys full of them," Michael countered.

"How can it thus be a hospitable place for the humans to come?"

"Abba will renew it before then," Michael answered. "It will be perfect once again, but I have the feeling He will have to renew it more than just occasionally."

Gabriel shook his head and then leaned back against a boulder. "And you loosened the gate for Lucifer. Surely, he will return to earth when he discovers how to use the portal."

Michael put his head down and rested his right hand against the same boulder. He was exhausted. "Abba's plan is that some do not remain locked within the gates of Hell forever - that these may roam throughout the earth, and that man must find a way, along his own path, to defeat them. Some will require our help to do so."

"It will be just like hell on earth for these humans, no?" Gabriel asked.

"I suppose it will be, especially for those who are not devoted and loyal to Abba," Michael answered with a bit of regret in his voice.

"Why must it be so?" Gabriel asked again, surprised.

"It is the will of Abba Himself that this battle never ends until He is ready for it to end. Until then, Abba intends to see if, and then also just how, man will use his free will to overcome Lucifer and his evil legions."

He looked at Gabriel, who seemed overwhelmed with concern. Gabriel unleashed his worries onto Michael. "If this battle has been so difficult for us to overcome, and we, his loyal angels; then mankind will surely have to struggle, with much pain along the way, throughout their time on earth."

"True, Gabriel, true." He exhaled a loud blast of air. "Turns out - Lucifer was jealous for no reason. We would have all had it much better if not for their turning against Abba."

"This must have been Abba's intentions all along," Gabriel concluded.

"Hard to say - only Abba, Yeshua, and Eliezer know this for sure." Michael stood upright and began walking. "C'mon, time for us to depart earth, *for now* — surely, we will be back and rather often. Abba means to send mankind much help along the way."

They came between two boulders and stood before a revolving circle of barely visible dust particles spinning in circles within a mild vortex of air.

Before entering the portal, Gabriel asked, "In what form will this help come?"

Michael looked at him with caring eyes, and in a confident tone, said, "Through you, me, and the various prophets he will rise up from out of all of mankind for those remaining loyal to Abba. Together with these prophets, we will come to man at his most grievous times, with messages we deliver to them from Abba. With the aid of our strength, and the interventions from the Triune in the form of guidance and wisdom, those who pray to Abba will receive His comfort."

Michael concluded by saying, *"Eliezer will always be with them should they call upon Him, and soon enough, Yeshua will have an extremely essential role that will last throughout mankind's history."*

Gabriel nodded, and with that, they entered the portal and moments later, had arrived back in Second Heaven ....

Afterword

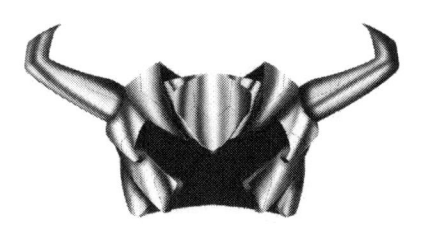

Thank you for reading.

It is my hope that my readers may have gleaned a little light and understanding for what has been, *and how what happened with Lucifer and his legions, still affects each of us even today.*

The truth of what actually occurred will be known to us someday. I hope I was close to it with this Book One, and the GAP Books to follow.

Perhaps, at that time, we may fully have the knowledge of why our history is littered with violence and dissatisfaction, which is further evidence of just how Lucifer is working in our world.

He has had the experience, the cunning, the time, tools, and the power necessary to sway some of us against God. Today, he is winning – just look out across the country anywhere. God is being less praised, observed, or even acknowledged as existing.

But for those of us who have faith and who devote a prayerful allotment and devotion to God, *we know who will be victorious once and for all when He is ready.* It may be easy to fall away from God, but life itself demands that we do not do so. Because then we become mere fodder for Lucifer.

I believe those who are truly loyal to Abba can never be tempted enough that they fall away from our one and only purpose, even though it may seem so at the worst of times. We had been meant for, created for, that which He had always hoped we would be from the very beginning of time itself: *God's beloved, devoted, and loyal brethren, and sons and daughters of Abba Himself.*

In Book Two, I further the story of how Lucifer plotted and planned while on earth, waiting in preparation for the birth of mankind, where he could finally strike back at the Heavenly Host once and for all. *This was why mankind was vulnerable right from the start.*

Table of Authorities

Editors and Staff of Bible Study Tools. (2022, March 13). *Archangel Michael in the Bible*. Retrieved from Bible Study Tools: https://www.biblestudytools.com/topical-verses/archangel-michael-in-the-bible/?amp

Editors and Staff of Catholic Online. (2022, February 20). *St. Gabriel, the Archangel*. Retrieved from Catholic Online: https://www.catholic.org/saints/saint.php?saint_id=279

Editors and Staff of Lignoma.com Magazine. (2021, January 31). *The Archangel Gabriel: everything worth knowing about this angel*. Retrieved from Lignoma.com Magazine: https://www.lignoma.com/en/magazine/archangel-gabriel-everything-worth-knowing/

McIver, T. (1988, September). *Formless and Void: Gap Theory Creationism*. Retrieved from National Center for Science Eduction. Creation/Evolution Journal: https://ncse.ngo/formless-and-void-gap-theory-creationism

Pilliod, M. (2017, February 9). *From the desk of Mr. Pilliod: The GAP Theory*. Retrieved from Crossroads Christian Academy, Secondary Principal's Blog: https://www.ccapanama.org/academics/the-gap-theory/

Stewart, D. (2021, September 15). *What Is the Gap Theory? (The Ruin and Reconstruction Theory?)*. Retrieved from Blue Letter Bible: https://www.blueletterbible.org/faq/don_stewart/don_stewart_654.cfm

Depictions of Shields, Weapons, and Armor:

This is the shield. Solid silver and gold. 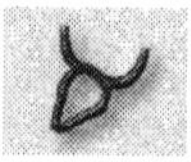 the aleph which is the first letter of the Hebrew alphabet is on the right side of the shield in gold. The Tav which is the Cross on the left side of the cross is the last letter of the Hebrew alphabet. Side note the bull head is what was offered as a sin offering in ancient Israel. The Tav, the Cross, Jesus, is the last sin offering to humans. The cross is on the left in silver. Hebrew is read right to left.

Helmet solid gold and silver

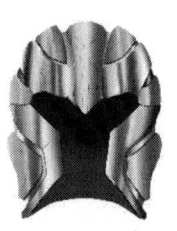

Armor solid gold and silver

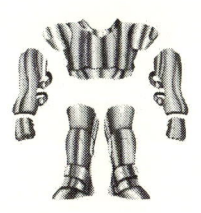

All the angels wore this while in heaven.

This is an Arrow. Arrowhead made up of Fire and Ice. The shaft is solid silver. The flight are solid gold.

This is an arrow quiver made of solid gold and silver

This is a sword. The blade is fire and ice. Hand is solid silver and gold